A TEEN'S GUIDE TO
FINANCIAL
LITERACY

A MATHEMATICAL
APPROACH

A TEEN'S GUIDE TO FINANCIAL LITERACY

A MATHEMATICAL APPROACH

FAWAZ SHARAF

ISBN: 978-1-78324-298-6

Book design by Wordzworth
www.wordzworth.com

This book is dedicated to His Majesty King Abdullah II of the Hashemite Kingdom of Jordan, whose visionary leadership and tireless dedication to the well-being and education of the younger generation inspires us all.

Contents

Introduction

Welcome to "A Teen's Guide to Financial Literacy: A Mathematical Approach," an introductory book (designed like a course) to teach fundamental financial concepts through the lens of mathematics and problem solving.

My primary aim is to empower you with the essential skills of financial literacy, by leveraging the power of mathematics as a dynamic tool to comprehend and navigate the world of money management. While some exercises in this book are intentionally straightforward, their primary purpose isn't to challenge you with mathematical complexity. Instead, they have been designed to introduce and reinforce fundamental financial terminology and concepts, so you can grasp the practical implications of everyday financial choices and how they can profoundly impact your short-term and long-term financial goals.

Throughout these pages, you will explore a wide range of financial topics including budgeting, saving, investing, debt management and retirement planning, all framed within the context of mathematical problem solving.

By choosing to embark on this book, you have taken a proactive step towards an early start on your journey to financial literacy and a brighter financial future. By the end of this book, you ought to feel more confident in your knowledge and ability to make more informed financial decisions.

I hope you enjoy this book.

Fawaz Sharaf

2023

UNIT 1

What is Financial Literacy?

Financial literacy refers to the knowledge and skills necessary to make informed and effective decisions about money management. It encompasses various areas such as budgeting, saving, investing, borrowing money and understanding financial products and services. Developing financial literacy can significantly impact your ability to make wise and sensible financial choices and achieve your short-term and long-term financial goals.

In order to effectively understand the world of personal finance, it is crucial to have a strong grasp of key terms and concepts. In this section, we will explore and define essential terms related to financial literacy. By familiarizing yourself with key terms, you can gain the confidence and knowledge to navigate financial situations, make informed decisions and protect yourself from potential financial pitfalls. Let's get started!

1.1 Key Terms

Financial Literacy: The knowledge and understanding of financial concepts and skills necessary to make informed financial decisions.

Personal Finance: The management of an individual's or a household's financial matters, including income, expenses, savings, investments and debt.

Financial Goal: An objective or target related to one's finances, such as saving for retirement, buying a house, or paying off debt.

Budget: A plan that outlines an individual's or organization's income and expenses over a specific period, typically monthly or yearly.

Income: The money received by an individual or organization, often in the form of a salary, wages, or profits.

Gross Income: The total income earned before any deductions or taxes are taken out.

Net Income: The income remaining after deducting taxes and other expenses from gross income.

Taxable Income: The portion of an individual's or business's income that is subject to taxation after allowable deductions and exemptions have been accounted for. It is the income on which taxes are calculated and paid.

Paycheck: A document issued by an employer to an employee, indicating the amount of money earned and deductions for taxes and other expenses.

Gratuity: A sum of money given voluntarily as a token of appreciation or goodwill for a service received. It is commonly associated with tipping in various service industries such as restaurants, hotels and personal services like hair salons or taxis.

Commission: A fee or compensation paid to an individual or entity for their services, usually based on a percentage of the total transaction value.

Credit: The ability to borrow money or obtain goods or services with the promise of paying back the lender or creditor at a later date.

Debt: Money owed to creditors or lenders as a result of borrowing funds or purchasing goods or services on credit.

Credit Score: A numerical representation of an individual's creditworthiness, which is used by lenders to assess the risk of extending credit.

Credit Report: A detailed record of an individual's credit history, their borrowing and repayment activities as well as their credit worthiness.

Credit Worthiness: A person's ability and likelihood to repay borrowed money or fulfill financial obligations.

Credit Limit: The maximum amount of money that a lender or financial institution is willing to extend as credit to an individual or business.

Identity Theft: The fraudulent acquisition and use of another person's personal information, typically for financial gain.

Interest: The cost of borrowing money or the return earned on savings or investments.

Compound Interest: Interest calculated on the initial principal and accumulated interest from previous periods.

Annual Percentage Rate (APR): The yearly interest generated by a sum that is charged to borrowers or paid to investors. It is expressed as a percentage that represents the yearly cost of funds over the term of a loan or income earned on an investment.

Insurance: A contract between an individual and an insurance company that provides financial protection against certain risks or losses.

Deductible: The amount that an individual must pay out-of-pocket before an insurance company covers the remaining costs.

Taxes: Mandatory fees imposed by the government on individuals and businesses to fund public services and programs.

Sales Tax: A tax imposed by the government on the sale of goods and services. It is usually a percentage of the purchase price and is collected by the seller at the point of sale.

Income Tax: A compulsory financial charge imposed by the government on individuals and businesses based on their income or profits. It is a percentage of one's earnings that must be paid to the government to fund public services and government operations.

Investment Income Tax: The taxes levied on various types of investment income such as capital gains, dividends and interest income.

Corporate Tax: A tax imposed on the profits earned by corporations or businesses. It is typically based on the company's taxable income, which is calculated by deducting allowable expenses from the total revenue.

Inheritance Tax: A tax imposed on the assets or property inherited by an individual after the death of the original owner. The tax is typically calculated based on the value of the inherited assets.

Capital Gains Tax: A tax imposed on the profits earned from the sale of certain assets such as stocks, real estate or valuable personal property. The tax is based on the difference between the purchase price (cost basis) and the selling price of the asset. It is designed to capture the gains made from the appreciation in the value of the asset over time.

Tax Deduction: A specific expense or cost that can be subtracted from an individual's or business's taxable income, resulting in a reduction of the total amount of tax owed.

Tax Credit: A direct reduction of the amount of tax owed to the government.

Income Tax Return: A form filed with a tax authority that reports income, deductions and credits to determine the amount of taxed owed or refunded.

Financial Institution: An organization that provides a range of financial services such as banking, lending, investing and insurance.

Checking Account: A bank account that allows individuals to deposit, withdraw and manage their funds for everyday transactions.

Check: A written order directing a bank to pay a specific amount of money from the account holder to a person/entity named in the check.

Certified Check: A personal check that is guaranteed by the check writer's bank.

Bank Draft/Manager's Check: Guaranteed funds payment instruments issued by a bank on the request of its customer (payer) to make a payment to a third party (payee).

Post-Dated Check: A check written by the payer for a future date.

Electronic Wire Transfer: A method of transferring money electronically from one person or institution to another using banking networks.

Non Sufficient Funds (NSF): When an account does not have enough money to cover a transaction.

Overdraft Protection: A service offered by banks allowing account holders to spend more than the amount in their account, preventing declined transactions due to insufficient funds.

Saving Account: A bank account designed for individuals to securely deposit and store their money while earning interest on the balance.

Credit Card: A card that allows the holder to make purchases on credit, with the obligation to repay the borrowed amount to the card issuer.

Debit Card: A payment card that you can use to make a purchase, with funds instantly deducted from the bank account it is linked to.

Loan: A financial arrangement where one party, typically a lender or financial institution, provides a specific amount of money to another party, known as the borrower. The borrower typically agrees to repay the loan amount over a set period of time, usually with interest.

Line of Credit: A loan arrangement from a financial institution that allows borrowers to draw funds up to a specified limit and repay them as needed, typically with interest.

Saving: Setting aside a portion of income or money for future use or emergencies.

Financial Planning: The process of setting and achieving financial goals by assessing one's current financial situation and creating a roadmap for the future.

Pension: A retirement plan that provides a monthly income during retirement.

Retirement Planning: The process of determining the financial goals and strategies needed to live comfortably during retirement years.

Estate Planning: The process of managing and distributing one's assets and wealth upon death, including wills, trusts, and power of attorney.

Will: A legal document that outlines a person's wishes regarding the distribution of their assets and the handling of their affairs after their death.

Net Worth: The difference between an individual's assets and liabilities, representing their overall financial position.

Equity: Ownership interest in an asset after deducting liabilities.

Capital: Financial resources, such as money or assets, used to generate income or investment returns.

Investment: Allocating money or resources with the expectation of generating income or increasing wealth over time.

Diversification: Spreading investments across different assets or securities to reduce risk.

Stocks/Shares: Securities that represent ownership in a company.

Securities: Tradable financial assets such as stocks and bonds.

Stock Market: A marketplace where shares of publicly traded companies are bought and sold.

Dividend: A distribution of a portion of a company's profits to its shareholders.

Mutual Fund: An investment vehicle that pools money from multiple investors to invest in a diversified portfolio of stocks, bonds, or other securities.

Annuity: A financial product that provides a series of payments over a specified period of time, often used for retirement planning.

Non-Fungible Token (NFT): A type of digital asset that represents ownership or proof of authenticity of a unique item or piece of content. NFTs are unique and cannot be exchanged on a like-for-like basis. NFTs are increasingly being used to represent digital artworks, collectibles, and other digital assets.

Cryptocurrency: Digital or virtual currency that uses cryptography for security and operates independently of a central bank. It is a decentralized form of currency that utilizes blockchain technology to secure transactions and verify the transfer of assets.

Mortgage: A loan provided by a bank or financial institution to purchase real estate, typically with the property serving as collateral.

Principal: The original sum of money invested or borrowed, excluding any interest or earnings.

Down payment: An initial payment made by a buyer towards the purchase of a large-ticket item, typically a house or a car.

Minimum Payment: The lowest amount that an individual or borrower must pay towards a debt or credit card balance to meet the payment obligation for a specific period.

Prepayment Penalty: A fee or charge imposed by a lender or financial institution when a borrower pays off a loan or debt before the agreed-upon maturity date.

Amortization: The process of gradually paying off a debt or loan over time through regular payments.

Capital Gain: The profit realized from the sale or disposal of a capital asset, such as stocks, bonds or real estate.

Capital Loss: The financial loss incurred when the selling price of a capital asset is lower than its original price.

Collateral: An asset or property offered as security to obtain a loan or credit.

Asset: An item owned by an individual, organization or entity, regarded as having economic value and/or future benefit.

Liability: An obligation or debt that an individual, organization, or entity owes to another party.

Risk: The potential for loss or negative outcomes associated with an investment or decision.

Cash Flow: The movement of money in and out of an individual's or organization's accounts over a specific period.

Liquidity: The ease with which an asset can be converted into cash without significant loss in value.

Return on Investment (ROI): A measure of the profitability of an investment, expressed as a percentage of the initial investment.

Budget Deficit: When a government's or individual's spending exceeds their income or revenue, resulting in a shortfall or negative balance.

Budget Surplus: When a government's or individual's income or revenue exceeds their spending, resulting in a positive balance or excess funds.

Fixed Cost: An expense that remains constant regardless of the level of production or sales volume.

Variable Cost: An expense that fluctuates in direct proportion to the level of production or sales volume.

Funds: Monetary resources or assets that are set aside or allocated for a specific purpose.

Costs: Amount paid for a purchase or expenditure, including the monetary value of resources used to produce or provide a good or service.

Capital Appreciation: The increase in value or worth of an asset over time.

Capital Depreciation: The decrease in value or worth of an asset over time.

Inventory: The collection of goods, products or materials that a business holds for sale, production or distribution.

Profit: The financial gain or positive difference between the revenue generated from business activities and the expenses incurred.

Loss: A negative financial outcome where the expenses or costs incurred exceed the revenue or income generated from a particular activity or business.

Revenue: The total amount of income generated by a business or organization from its core operations.

Expenses: Money spent or costs incurred in an organization's or individual's efforts to generate revenue, representing the cost of doing business.

Startup Costs: The expenses incurred by a new business at its inception or when launching a new product or service. These costs typically include expenses such as equipment purchases, marketing and advertising costs, legal fees, lease or rental payments and initial inventory.

Employee: An individual who is hired by an employer to perform specific tasks or work in exchange for wages or salary.

Employer: An individual or organization that hires and employs workers or employees to carry out specific tasks or work in exchange for wages or salary.

Entrepreneur: An individual who starts and operates a business, taking on financial risks in the hope of making profits.

Entrepreneurship: The process of starting and running a business, taking on financial risks in the hopes of making a profit.

Corporation: A legal entity separate from its partners, known as shareholders or stockholders. It is formed through a legal process called incorporation and is created to conduct business activities.

Partnership: A partnership is a legal form of business organization where two or more individuals, known as partners, come together to carry out a business venture for profit.

Sole Proprietorship: A sole proprietorship is the simplest form of business ownership and refers to a business that is owned and operated by a single individual and generally the owner is personally responsible for all aspects of the business including its debts and liabilities.

Capital Gains: The profits earned from the sale of a capital asset, such as stocks, bonds, real estate or valuable collectibles. It represents the difference between the purchase price and the selling price of the asset.

Capital Loss: A financial loss incurred when the selling price of an investment or asset is lower than its original purchase price. It occurs when the value of the investment or asset decreases over time.

Balance Sheet: A financial statement that provides a snapshot of a company's financial position at a specific point in time.

Income Statement: Also known as a profit and loss statement or statement of earnings; it is a financial statement that summarizes a company's revenues, expenses, gains and losses over a specific period of time.

Cash Flow Statement: Provides an overview of the company's cash flows from operating, investing and financing activities.

Bankruptcy: A legal process that allows individuals or businesses unable to repay their debts to seek relief from their financial obligations.

Recession: A period of temporary economic decline.

Inflation: The rate at which the general level of prices for goods and services rises, eroding the purchasing power of currency.

Deflation: A decrease in the general price level of goods and services in an economy over a period of time, resulting in an increase in the purchasing power of money.

Bear Market: A period of declining prices and negative investor sentiment in the financial market.

Bull Market: A period of time in the financial market when prices are generally rising, investor confidence is high and there is an optimistic outlook for future price gains.

1.2 Quiz

1 What is debt?

   A The ability to borrow money or obtain goods or services

   B The money spent on goods and services

   C Allocating money for future use or emergencies

   D Money owed to creditors or lenders

2 What is interest?

   A The money spent on goods and services

   B The cost of borrowing money or return earned on investments

   C The ability to borrow money or obtain goods or services

   D Allocating money for future use or emergencies

3 What is a budget?

    A The money received by an individual or organization

    B The money spent on goods and services

    C A plan that outlines income and expenses

    D The process of paying back a loan

4 What is a credit score used for?

    A Assessing the risk of extending credit

    B Allocating money for future use or emergencies

    C The money received by an individual or organization

    D The money spent on goods and services

5 What is the definition of income?

    A The cost of borrowing money from a bank

    B The money spent on goods and services

    C A plan that outlines income and expenses

    D The money received by an individual or organization, often in the form of a salary, wages, or profits

6 What does saving involve?

    A Allocating money for future use or emergencies

    B Prioritizing short-term wants over long-term financial goals

    C Spreading investments across different assets

    D The ability to borrow money or obtain goods or services

7 What is credit?

   A   The ability to borrow money or obtain goods or services with the promise of paying back the lender or creditor

   B   The cost of borrowing money

   C   The money spent on goods and services

   D   The process of gradually paying off a debt

8 What are expenses?

   A   The cost of borrowing money

   B   The money received by an individual or organization

   C   The money spent on goods and services

   D   A plan that outlines income and expenses

9 What is an investment?

   A   Allocating money for future use or emergencies

   B   The process of gradually paying off a debt

   C   The cost of borrowing money

   D   Allocating money with the expectation of generating income or increasing wealth

10 What is identity theft?

   A   The process of gradually paying off a debt through money borrowed from your friend

   B   The fraudulent acquisition and use of another person's personal information

   C   The money spent on goods and services using a credit card

   D   The process of starting and running a business using money borrowed from your parents

11 What is compound interest?

    A   Interest calculated on the initial principal only

    B   Interest calculated on the initial principal and accumulated interest from previous periods

    C   Interest charged by your landlord for paying your rent late

    D   The ability to obtain goods or services without immediate payment

12 What is insurance?

    A   Allocating money for future use or emergencies

    B   The process of gradually paying off a debt

    C   A contract that provides financial protection against risks or losses

    D   The ability to obtain goods or services without immediate payment

13 What is diversification?

    A   The process of gradually paying off a debt

    B   The ability to obtain goods or services without immediate payment

    C   Allocating money across different assets to reduce risk

    D   The process of starting and running a business

14 What is entrepreneurship?

    A   Allocating money for future use or emergencies

    B   The process of gradually paying off a debt

    C   The ability to borrow money or obtain goods or services

    D   The process of starting and running a business

15 What is gross income?

    A The total income earned before deductions or taxes

    B The total income earned after deductions and taxes

    C The money spent on goods and services

    D Tho proocoo of gradually paylriy uff a aebt

16 What is net income?

    A The total income earned before deductions or taxes

    B The total income earned after deductions and taxes

    C The money spent on goods and services

    D The process of gradually paying off a debt

17 What is inflation?

    A The rate at which the general level of prices rises

    B The ability to obtain goods or services without immediate payment

    C The process of gradually paying off a debt

    D Allocating money for future use or emergencies

18 Where are shares of publicly traded companies bought and sold?

    A Real estate market

    B Stock market

    C Bond market

    D Credit market

19 What is financial planning?

    A The process of gradually paying off a debt

    B The process of setting and achieving financial goals

    C The ability to obtain goods or services without immediate payment

    D Allocating money across different assets to commit tax fraud

20 What is commission?

    A   A tax levied on goods and services

    B   A salary paid to an employee

    C   A fee or compensation for services rendered

    D   An interest charged on borrowing money

21 What is a paycheck?

    A   The taxes paid by an individual or organization

    B   The process of gradually paying off a debt

    C   The ability to obtain goods or services without immediate payment

    D   A document indicating the amount of money earned and deductions

22 What are taxes?

    A   The process of gradually paying off a debt

    B   The ability to obtain goods or services without immediate payment

    C   The cost of borrowing money

    D   Mandatory fees imposed by the government to fund public services

23 What is retirement planning?

    A   The process of gradually paying off a debt after retirement

    B   The ability to obtain goods or services without immediate payment

    C   The process of setting and achieving financial goals for retirement

    D   The money spent on goods and services during retirement

24 What is a mortgage?

    A   A loan to purchase real estate

    B   The process of gradually paying off a debt

    C   The ability to obtain goods or services without immediate paymont

    D   The money spent on goods and services

25 What is a credit card?

    A   A loan to purchase real estate

    B   The process of gradually paying off a debt

    C   A card allowing purchases on credit

    D   A card that instantly transfers funds from your bank account

26 What is financial literacy?

    A   The knowledge and understanding of financial concepts and skills

    B   The process of gradually paying off a debt

    C   The ability to obtain goods or services without immediate payment

    D   The process of distributing your assets

27 What is estate planning?

    A   The process of gradually paying off a debt

    B   The ability to obtain goods or services without immediate payment

    C   The management and distribution of assets upon death

    D   The knowledge and understanding of financial concepts and skills

28 What is an asset?

    A   The process of gradually paying off a debt

    B   An item or property of value that is owned by a person or company

    C   The ability to obtain goods or services without immediate payment

    D   The management and distribution of assets upon death

29 What is a liability?

    A   The process of gradually paying off a debt

    B   Anything of value that is owned

    C   An obligation or debt owed

    D   The management and distribution of assets upon death

30 What is net worth?

    A   The process of gradually paying off a debt

    B   The value of assets minus liabilities

    C   An obligation or debt owed

    D   The management and distribution of assets upon death

31 What is financial risk?

    A   The process of gradually paying off a debt

    B   The potential for loss or negative financial outcomes

    C   When you obtain a property assessment

    D   The process of preparing a will

32 What is cash flow?

    A   The process of gradually paying off a debt

    B   The movement of money in and out of accounts

    C   An obligation or debt owed

    D   The management and distribution of assets upon death

33 What is liquidity?

    A The process of gradually paying off a debt

    B The process of obtaining a mortgage

    C The ease of converting an asset into cash

    D The ability to obtain goods or services without immediate payment

34 What is bankruptcy?

    A The process of gradually paying off a debt

    B The ability to obtain goods or services without immediate payment

    C The legal relief from financial obligations when unable to repay debts

    D The knowledge and understanding of financial concepts and skills

35 What is amortization?

    A The process of gradually paying off a debt

    B The original sum of money invested or borrowed

    C The cost of borrowing money

    D The ability to obtain goods or services without immediate payment

36 What is a dividend?

    A The annualized interest rate charged on borrowed money

    B A distribution of a company's profits to shareholders

    C The cost of borrowing money

    D The ability to obtain goods or services without immediate payment

37 What is capital?

A   The annualized interest rate charged on borrowed money

B   Financial resources used to generate income or returns

C   The cost of borrowing money

D   The ability to obtain goods or services without immediate payment

38 What is principal?

A   The annualized interest rate charged on borrowed money

B   The original sum of money invested or borrowed

C   The cost of borrowing money

D   The ability to obtain goods or services without immediate payment

39 What is a mutual fund?

A   An investment vehicle that pools money from multiple investors to invest in securities

B   The original sum of money invested or borrowed

C   The cost of borrowing money

D   The ability to obtain goods or services without immediate payment

40 What is a stock?

A   A share of ownership in a company

B   The original sum of money invested or borrowed

C   The cost of borrowing money

D   The ability to obtain goods or services without immediate payment

41 What is a bond?

    A A debt security issued by a government or corporation

    B The original sum of money invested or borrowed

    C The cost of borrowing money

    D The ability to obtain goods or services without immediate payment

42 What is a bear market?

    A A market condition characterized by rising prices and optimism

    B The original sum of money invested or borrowed

    C The cost of borrowing money

    D A market condition characterized by falling prices and pessimism

43 What is a bull market?

    A A market condition characterized by rising prices and optimism

    B The original sum of money invested or borrowed

    C A market condition characterized by falling prices and pessimism

    D The ability to obtain goods or services without immediate payment

44 What is a budget deficit?

    A The original sum of money invested or borrowed

    B A situation where expenses exceed income

    C A situation where income exceeds expenses

    D The ability to obtain goods or services without immediate payment

45 What is a budget surplus?

    A   A situation where income exceeds expenses

    B   The original sum of money invested or borrowed

    C   A situation where expenses exceed income

    D   The ability to obtain goods or services without immediate payment

46 What is a will?

    A   The ability to obtain goods or services without immediate payment

    B   A contract outlining the original sum of money invested or borrowed

    C   A legal document outlining the cost of borrowing money

    D   A legal document that specifies how a person's assets should be distributed upon death

47 What is a checking account?

    A   A bank account for day-to-day transactions

    B   A bank account for storing money and earning interest

    C   The cost of borrowing money

    D   The ability to obtain goods or services without immediate payment

48 What is a savings account?

    A   A bank account for storing money and earning interest

    B   The original sum of money invested or borrowed

    C   A bank account for day-to-day transactions

    D   The ability to obtain goods or services without immediate payment

49 What is a credit report?

    A   The ability to obtain goods or services without immediate payment

    B   A report summarizing the original sum of money invested or borrowed

    C   The cost of borrowing money

    D   A document that contains an individual's credit history and creditworthiness

50 What is a financial institution?

    A   A university that offers scholarships to its students

    B   The original sum of money invested or borrowed

    C   An organization that provides financial services such as banking and investing

    D   The ability to obtain goods or services without immediate payment

51 What is a down payment?

    A   A portion of the purchase price paid upfront when buying an item or property

    B   The original sum of money invested or borrowed

    C   The cost of borrowing money

    D   The ability to obtain goods or services without immediate payment

52 What is a credit limit?

    A   The cost of borrowing money

    B   The original sum of money invested or borrowed

    C   The maximum amount of credit available to a borrower

    D   The ability to obtain goods or services without immediate payment

53 What is a minimum payment?

    A   The original sum of money invested or borrowed

    B   The lowest amount required to be paid on a credit card balance to avoid late fees

    C   The cost of borrowing money at a low interest rate

    D   The ability to obtain goods or services without immediate payment

54 What is a tax deduction?

    A   An expense that reduces taxable income

    B   The original sum of money invested or borrowed

    C   The cost of borrowing money

    D   The amount of tax owed from investments

55 What is a tax credit?

    A   A dollar-for-dollar reduction of the tax owed

    B   A type of loan provided by the government to help individuals pay their taxes

    C   The cost of borrowing money

    D   The maximum amount of income an individual can earn before being subject to taxes

56 What is a prepayment penalty?

    A   A penalty fee for borrowing money

    B   The original sum of money invested or borrowed

    C   A fee charged for paying off a loan before the designated term

    D   The ability to obtain goods or services without immediate payment

57 What is a capital gain?

    A   The profit from the sale of an investment

    B   The original sum of money invested or borrowed

    C   The cost of borrowing money

    D   The ability to obtain goods or services without immediate payment

58 What is a capital loss?

    A   The loss from the sale of an investment

    B   The original sum of money invested or borrowed

    C   The cost of borrowing money

    D   The ability to obtain goods or services without immediate payment

59 What is revenue?

    A   The total amount of expenses incurred by a business

    B   The total amount of money invested in a business

    C   The total amount of income generated by a business

    D   The total amount of assets owned by a business

60 What is a loan?

    A   The total amount of money invested in a business

    B   A financial arrangement where one party provides money to another party with the expectation of repayment

    C   The total amount of income generated by a business

    D   The total amount of expenses incurred by a business

61 What is capital appreciation?

    A   The increase in value or worth of an asset over time

    B   A financial arrangement where one party provides money to another party with the expectation of repayment

    C   The total amount of income generated by a business

    D   The process of evaluating the performance of an employee

62 What is capital depreciation?

    A   The increase in value or worth of an asset over time

    B   The process of evaluating the performance of an employee

    C   The decrease in value or worth of an asset over time

    D   The total amount of expenses incurred by a business

63 What is inventory?

    A   The total amount of money invested in a business

    B   The collection of goods, products or materials that a business holds for sale, production or distribution

    C   The total amount of income generated by a business

    D   The decrease in value of an asset over time

64 What is personal finance?

    A   The total amount of money invested in a business

    B   The process of filing personal income tax returns

    C   The total amount of income generated by a business

    D   The management of an individual's or household's financial matters

65 What is sales tax?

- **A** A tax imposed on income earned by individuals
- **B** A tax imposed on the sale of goods and services
- **C** A tax imposed on property ownership
- **D** A tax imposed on inherited property

66 What is income tax?

- **A** A tax imposed on goods and services purchased
- **B** A tax levied on the profits of businesses
- **C** A tax imposed on property and real estate
- **D** A tax levied on an individual's or business's income

67 What is corporate tax?

- **A** A tax imposed on inventory purchased by a company
- **B** A tax imposed on profits earned by corporations
- **C** A tax imposed by businesses on sales of goods and services to consumers
- **D** A tax imposed on property ownership

68 What is taxable income?

- **A** The total income earned by an individual or business before any deductions and exemptions
- **B** Gifts received from family and friends
- **C** Income that is subject to taxation after deducting allowable expenses and exemptions
- **D** Education expenses

69 What is profit?

    A   The increase in value of an asset

    B   The amount of money left after deducting expenses from revenue

    C   The initial investment made to start a business

    D   The value of assets owned by a business

70 What is a gratuity?

    A   A mandatory fee charged by service providers

    B   A sum of money given voluntarily as a token of appreciation

    C   A discount offered on a product or service

    D   A type of tax levied on restaurant bills

71 What is investment income tax?

    A   Tax on the purchase of investment assets

    B   Tax on the income or gains from investments

    C   Tax on the financial institution managing the investments

    D   Tax on the amount invested in a specific asset

72 What is inheritance tax?

    A   A tax on the income from investments

    B   A tax on gifts given during a person's lifetime

    C   A tax on assets inherited after the death of the original owner

    D   A tax on the purchase of goods and services

73 What is capital gains tax?

    A   A tax on the total income earned from all sources

    B   A tax on the profits earned from the sale of assets

    C   A tax on the salary and wages earned by individuals

    D   A tax on the interest earned from bank savings accounts

74 Your equity in a home increases if you:

    A   Take out a larger mortgage loan

    B   Miss a mortgage payment

    C   Make home improvements that increase its value

    D   Allow the property to fall into despair

75 What is an employee?

    A   An individual who owns and operates a business

    B   An individual who provides services to clients on a contractual basis

    C   An individual who is hired by an employer to perform work

    D   An individual who invests in stocks and bonds for financial gain

76 What is an employer?

    A   An individual who provides service to clients on a contractual basis

    B   An individual who invests in stocks and bonds for financial gain

    C   A business that hires employees

    D   A volunteer group that cleans up city parks

77 During a recession it is common to observe:

    A   Rapid job growth

    B   Falling stock market prices

    C   A boom in luxury goods sales

    D   An increase in making high-risk investments

78 What is an entrepreneur?

    A   An individual who works as an employee in a large corporation

    B   A student who works part-time on campus

    C   An individual who starts and operates their own business, taking on financial risks

    D   A company that provides consulting services to other businesses

79 What is a variable cost?

    A   An expense that remains constant regardless of the level of production or sales volume

    B   An expense that fluctuates based on the level of production or sales volume

    C   Costs associated with salaries of permanent employees

    D   Rental costs for business premises

80 What is cryptocurrency?

    A   A digital or virtual form of currency that uses cryptography for security

    B   Physical coins and notes issued by a central bank

    C   A centralized currency system controlled by a government

    D   A type of investment fund managed by financial institutions

81 What is a fixed cost?

    A   An expense that varies based on the level of production or sales volume

    B   An expense that remains constant regardless of the level of production or sales volume

    C   A cost associated with sales commissions

    D   A cost incurred only during the initial setup of a business

82 A balance sheet is a financial statement that summarizes a company's revenues, expenses, gains and losses over a specific period of time.

    A   True

    B   False

83 An annuity is an investment vehicle that pools money from multiple investors to invest in a diversified portfolio of stocks, bonds, or other securities.

    A   True

    B   False

84 Diversification represents the process of gradually paying off a debt or loan over time through regular payments.

    A   True

    B   False

85 Return on Investment represents the yearly interest generated by a sum that is charged to borrowers or paid to investors.

    A   True

    B   False

86 A partnership is a legal form of business organization where two or more individuals, known as partners, come together to carry out a business venture for profit.

A True

B False

87 Using leverage in financial investments means utilizing borrowed money to increase potential returns.

A True

B False

88 Accruing debt always indicates that a business is in poor financial health.

A True

B False

89 A bank draft represents a guaranteed funds payment instrument.

A True

B False

90 A Manager's Check offers a bank account holder overdraft protection in case of insufficient funds in an account.

A True

B False

UNIT 2

Making Informed Purchasing Decisions

In this section, we will delve into math problems designed to sharpen your decision-making abilities. We will explore topics such as calculating discounts and sale prices, determining the better unit price for a product, evaluating the financial feasibility of repairing or replacing an item, and assessing the value of purchasing add-ons like warranties or insurance. We will also explore the realm of membership fees versus single-use costs to determine which payment structure offers the most financial advantage. Through these exercises you can develop a keen understanding of the long-term financial impact of your purchasing decisions.

2.1 Discounts and Sale Prices

There are various types of store discounts including, two-for-one, buy one, get one free and percentage discounts. By practicing the following questions, you can learn how to spot and calculate the best deals and make savvy purchasing decisions.

Typically, a store will discount an item by a percentage of the original price. The discount rate is usually given as a percentage. To find the discount, multiply the discount rate by the original price. To find the sale price, subtract the discount from the original price.

The first one has been solved for you!

1 A video game console is originally priced at $300, and there is a 10% discount. What is the sale price?

SOLUTION

Step 1: Calculate the discount

Discount = 10% *of* $300 = 0.10 x $300 = $30

Step 2: Calculate the sale price

Sale price = *Original price - Discount* = $300 - $30 = $270

(You can also calculate the sale price this way: $300 x 0.90)

Now try the next questions on your own!

2   A pair of sunglasses is originally priced at $120, and there is a 15% discount. What is the sale price?

3   A laptop is originally priced at $900, and there is a 25% discount. What is the sale price?

4   A bicycle is originally priced at $400, but there is a 20% discount. What is the sale price?

5   A pair of boots is originally priced at $150, and there is a 30% discount. What is the sale price?

6   An item is on sale for 30% off its original price of $90. What is the sale price of the item?

7   An item is on sale for 25% off its original price of $150. What is the sale price of the item?

8   An item is on sale for 25% off its original price of $120. What is the sale price of the item?

9   Store A offers a coupon for 25% off the original price, and Store B offers a coupon for $10 off the original price. If the original price is $80, which coupon offers a better deal?

10   Store E offers a coupon for $5 off any purchase, and Store F offers a coupon for 20% off the original price. If the original price is $30, which coupon offers a better deal?

11   Store G offers a coupon for 40% off the original price, and Store H offers a coupon for $15 off the original price. If the original price is $50, which coupon offers a better deal?

12   Store I offers a coupon for 10% off the original price, and Store J offers a coupon for $8 off the original price. If the original price is $70, which coupon offers a better deal?

13   Store A offers a coupon for 25% off the original price, Store B offers a coupon for $15 off the original price, and Store C offers a coupon for 10% off the original price. If the original price is $80, which coupon saves you the most money? Calculate the final price for each store after applying the coupon.

14 You purchase the same shampoo monthly and are comparing four-month promotions at the following stores. Store X offers a coupon for 30% off the original price, Store Y offers a coupon for $20 off the original price, and Store Z offers a "buy one, get one free" coupon. If the original price is $120, which coupon saves you the most money during the four-month promotion? Calculate the final price for each store after applying the coupon.

15 A store has a "buy 1 get 1 free" offer on shampoos. The original price of the shampoo is $50. How much money do you save by taking advantage of this deal?

16 Lucy purchased a sweater for $132 on sale, when the regular price was $220. What was the rate of discount?

17 The sale price of a used Geography textbook after a discount of 20% was $110. What was the regular price of the book?

18 In a boutique, an evening gown is on sale for $80. The original price of the gown was $100. What is the rate of discount?

19 A store offers a coupon that gives you $5 back on a purchase of $25 or more. If you buy $40 worth of items, how much money will you save with the coupon?

20 A store offers a coupon that gives you 15% cash back on your total purchase. If you spend $200, how much money will you save with the coupon?

21 A store offers a coupon that gives you $10 back for every $50 spent. If you spend $120, how much money will you get back?

22 A store offers a coupon that gives you 20% cash back on your total purchase. If you spend $80, how much money will you get back?

23 Store A offers a promotion where you can buy 3 items for $20. Store B offers a promotion where you can buy 5 items for $35. Which store offers a better deal in terms of the price per item?

24 Store A offers a promotion where you can buy 2 items for $12. Store B offers a promotion where you can buy 4 items for $26. Which store offers a better deal in terms of the price per item?

2.2 Unit Price and Converting Units of Measure

Engaging in math problems that focus on calculating unit prices and converting units of measure can equip you with valuable skills to make informed purchasing decisions. By determining the unit price of a product, you can compare different package sizes or brands to find the best value for your money.

The first unit of measure conversion question has been solved for you.

1 A 2-gallon jug of orange juice costs $9.60. What is the price per quart?

SOLUTION

Step 1: Convert from gallons to quarts. (1 gallon = 4 quarts)

2 x 4 *quarts* = 8 *quarts*

Step 2: Divide the total price by 8. $9.60/8 = $1.20

The price per quart = $1.20

Now try the rest of these questions.

2 A 4–yard roll of yarn costs $4.80. What is the price per foot? (1 yard = 3 feet)

3 A 4-foot roll of aluminum foil costs $0.96. What is the price per inch? (1 foot = 12 inches)

4 A 2-quart carton of milk costs $2.80. What is the price per cup? (1 quart = 4 cups)

5   3 pounds of chicken costs $2.40. What is the price per ounce? (1 pound = 16 ounces)

6   A package of 500g of rice costs $3.50. What is the price per kilogram? (1,000 g = 1 kg)

7   A pack of 250ml juice costs $1.80. What is the unit price per liter? (1,000 ml = 1 L)

8   A bag of apples weighing 3 pounds costs $2.99. What is the unit price per kilogram? (1 pound = 0.45359237 kilograms)

9   A bottle of orange juice containing 1.5 liters costs $1.99. What is the unit price per gallon? (1 liter = 0.2641720524 gallons)

10 2 tons of soil cost $4,000. What is the price per pound? (1 ton = 2,000 pounds)

11 A 3-gallon container of paint costs $53.20. What is the price per quart? (1 gallon = 4 quarts)

2.3 Comparing Offers

Now try these. Which offer is better?

1   At Supermart ABC, a pack of 12 pens costs $3.60, while at PenMart, a pack of 6 pens costs $1.80. Which store offers the better unit price per pen?

2   At BestBakery, a box of 24 cookies costs $12. At CookieHeaven, a box of 16 cookies costs $8. Which store offers the better unit price per cookie?

3   At FreshFarm, a 2-pound bag of apples costs $3. At FruitMart, a 5-pound bag of apples costs $7. Which store offers the better price per pound?

4   At MegaMart, a 16-ounce bottle of shampoo costs $4. At SuperSaver, a 12-ounce bottle of shampoo costs $3. Which store offers the better price per ounce?

5   At SportsGear, a pack of 10 tennis balls costs $15. At PlayPro, a pack of 6 tennis balls costs $10. Which store offers the better price per tennis ball?

6   At BookMart, a 200-page notebook costs $2. At StationeryWorld, a 100-page notebook costs $1. Which store offers the better price per page?

7   At CoffeeHouse, a 12-ounce bag of coffee costs $8. At BrewCafe, a 16-ounce bag of coffee costs $12. Which store offers the better price per ounce?

8   At MovieZone, a 2-hour movie rental costs $4. At FlixNow, a 3-hour movie rental costs $6. Which store offers the better price per hour?

2.4 Comparing Options

1   Jenna is considering purchasing a music streaming service. The service offers two options: a monthly subscription plan for $19.99 or the option to purchase individual songs for $1.29 each. If Jenna typically listens to 16 songs per month, which option is more financially sensible for her?

2   Emily is an avid reader and is deciding between two options for accessing books. Option 1 is a monthly book subscription service that costs $19.99 per month, allowing her to borrow up to 5 books, plus $1.25 per additional book. Option 2 is purchasing books individually for $2.99 per book. If Emily reads 8 books per month, which option is more financially sensible for her?

3   Alex wants to watch movies regularly. He can either rent movies from a local rental store for $2.49 per movie or subscribe to a streaming service for $15 per month. If Alex watches 6 movies per month, which option costs less?

4 Amy enjoys going to the gym to work out. She can either pay $30 per month for a gym membership or pay $2.25 for a daily pass each time she goes to the gym. If Amy goes to the gym three times a week, which option will be more cost effective?

5 Susie has a laptop that is not working properly. She can either repair it for $150 or buy a new one for $800. The expected lifespan of the repaired laptop is 3 years, while the new laptop is expected to last for 5 years. Which option has a lower cost per year?

6 Mark wants to purchase a bike. He finds a used bike for $200, but it requires repairs costing $50. Alternatively, he can buy a brand new bike for $350. How much money can Mark save by buying the used bike and getting it repaired?

7 Amy spends $50 per month on cable TV subscription. She found a streaming service that costs $10 per month. How much money can Amy save per year by switching to the streaming service?

8 Jake is considering buying a hair dryer. The cost of a hair dryer is $40, and he estimates that it will last for 2 years. Alternatively, he can go to a hair salon and pay $1 per visit for blow drying, with an average of 2 visits per month. Which option is more cost-effective over a period of two years?

9 Michael is considering joining a gym. The gym offers monthly memberships for $50 or annual memberships for $500. Calculate the cost per month for each option and determine which one is more cost-effective.

10 Sarah drinks coffee five times a week. Sarah spends $3.65 on coffee from a café, five days a week. She wants to save money by making coffee at home instead. If she buys a bag of coffee beans at a cost of $10 to make 5 cups of coffee, how much can Sarah save in a month by brewing her own coffee?

11 Sam wants to compare meal options. The total cost of ingredients to cook breakfast, lunch and dinner for seven days is $375. Eating at restaurants costs $20 per meal plus 5% tip, and ordering food delivery costs $30 per meal plus 2% tax. If Sam eats three meals a day, which option is the most cost-effective per week?

Let's Explore

12 Emily is heading off to college and needs a reliable laptop for her studies. She finds one for $1,000 and is offered a 4-year extended warranty for $150. The warranty covers all repairs and includes one-time accidental damage replacement. Emily knows she will use the laptop extensively for her coursework and projects. She estimates a 60% chance of needing repairs and encountering damage during her college years. Determine whether Emily ought to purchase the warranty.

13 Sarah replaces her mobile phone every year. She plans to buy a new one for $800. The store is offering an extended warranty for an additional $175, to cover any repairs and replacements for the next two years. Should she purchase the warranty?

14 Tom and Lisa are moving into a new home and need to purchase a refrigerator, a washer and a dryer. Each appliance costs $800. The store offers a bundle warranty for all three appliances for $200, covering repairs and replacements for five years. While they are generally careful with their appliances, Tom and Lisa recognize that appliances may need repairs. They estimate a combined 10% chance of needing repairs on any of the appliances in the next five years. Determine whether they should purchase the bundle warranty.

2.5 Square Footage Price and Property Comparison

Understanding the price per square foot or meter is crucial when buying or selling property or land. This metric allows you to make informed decisions based on objective measurements. Here are several reasons why this is important.

- Effective Comparison: By calculating the cost per square foot or meter, you can directly compare properties.

- Identifying Trends: Tracking the cost per square foot/meter over time can help you spot trends in the real estate market and plan a purchase or sale strategically.

- Informed Negotiation: Knowing the cost per square foot/meter can empower you during purchase or sale negotiations.

- Investment Decisions: As a real estate investor, understanding the cost per square foot/meter can allow you to evaluate the potential return on investment and estimate overall profitability more accurately.

- Avoiding Overpaying: Without a grasp of this metric, you might unknowingly overpay for a property that appears appropriately priced, but is actually priced too high relative to its size or location.

- Projecting Expenses: When renovating or making additions to a property, knowing the cost per square foot/meter can help you estimate expenses and determine whether the project aligns with your budget and potential resale value.

In sum, understanding the price or cost per square foot/meter is a fundamental aspect of making well-informed decisions in the real estate market.

Now, let's calculate the price per square foot/meter in the following problems.

1   You are considering purchasing one of two properties. Casablanca has an area of 1,500 square feet and is priced at $300,000. Willows Creek has an area of 1,800 square feet and is priced at $360,000. Calculate the price per square foot for each property and determine which property has a lower price per square foot.

2   Joe is looking at three properties:

Property 1: 1,200 sq feet and priced at $240,000

Property 2: 2,800 sq feet and priced at $470,000

Property 3: 1,500 sq feet and priced at $315,000

Calculate the price per square foot for each property and determine which property offers the best value based on lowest price per square foot.

3   Emmanuel wants to purchase land that costs $250 per square meter. The land is 10,000 square feet in total. How much will Emmanuel have to pay to purchase the land? (1 sq meter = 10.764 sq ft)

4   Ayan is considering purchasing an apartment. Apartment A is priced at $200 per square meter and Apartment B is priced at $20 per square foot. Which apartment has a lower price per square foot? (1 sq meter = 10.764 sq ft)

5   You own an apartment that has an area of 150 square meters. The property management company charges a service fee of AED 14 per square foot for the maintenance of common areas. Calculate the total service charge you need to pay. (1 sq meter = 10.764 sq ft)

6   Rihanna wants to purchase a condo for 500,000 Euros. The annual service charge is 14 Euros per square foot. (a) If the condo is 450 square feet, how much will Rihanna pay in service charges annually? (b) How much will she pay the real estate agent, who charges a 2% commission based on the purchase price?

7   Taylor wants to rent a 250 square meter apartment for 27,650 AED. The landlord wants her to pay the annual service charge of 10 AED per square meter. (a) How much in service charges will she have to pay? (b) If the real estate agent charges the landlord a 5% commission based on the rental amount, how much will the landlord pay to the agent?

2.6 Currency Exchanges

Understanding how to calculate currency exchanges when traveling or purchasing an item online in a foreign currency ensures that you are aware of the actual cost and can make informed decisions about the value of the products or services you are purchasing. Note: The exchange rates and values used in the following questions are fictional. Actual exchange rates may vary.

The following question has been solved for you.

1   Ahmed from the UAE is visiting London and wants to buy a souvenir that costs £45. The exchange rate is 1 GBP = 4.50 AED. How much will Ahmed pay in AED?

SOLUTION

Since 1 GB = 4.50 AED, Ahmed must multiply the price by 4.50 AED/GBP.

Therefore, Ahmed will pay GBP 45 x 4.50 AED/GBP = AED 202.50.

Now try these questions.

2   Sara exchanged 400 UAE dirhams (AED) to British pounds (GBP) at an exchange rate of 1 GBP = 4.25 AED. How much GBP did Sara receive?

3   Omar converted 1,250 AED to GBP and received 250 GBP. What is 1 AED worth?

4   Aisha is traveling from the UAE to London with 1,500 AED. If the exchange rate is 1 GBP = 4.75 AED, how much in GBP will Aisha have after the conversion?

5   Mohammad bought a pair of shoes in London for £150. If the exchange rate is 1 GBP = 4.60 AED, how much did Mohammad spend in AED?

6   Fatima from Nigeria is traveling to the United States with 20,000 NGN. The exchange rate is 1 US dollar (USD) = 400 NGN. How much will Fatima receive in USD after the conversion?

7   Samuel exchanged 500,000 Nigerian naira (NGN) to USD and received 1,500 USD. How much is 1 NGN worth?

8   Tunde wants to buy a laptop in the US for $1,200. If the exchange rate is 1 USD = 410 NGN, how much will Tunde pay in NGN?

9   Sarah exchanged 1,000,000 NGN to USD at an exchange rate of 1 USD = 380 NGN. How much USD did Sarah receive?

10 If the exchange rate is 1 USD = 440 NGN, how much NGN would you receive for $500?

11 Emily is traveling from Canada to Jordan with 1,500 CAD. If the exchange rate is 1 CAD = 0.57 Jordanian dinars (JOD), how many JOD will Emily have after the conversion?

12 James exchanged 10,000 CAD to JOD and received 4,250 JOD. How much is 1 CAD worth relative to JOD?

13 Chloe wants to buy a traditional Jordanian outfit in Amman for 80 JOD. If the exchange rate is 1 CAD = 0.43 JOD, how much will Chloe spend in CAD?

14 David exchanged 2,000 CAD to JOD at an exchange rate of 1 CAD = 0.50 JOD. How much in JOD did David receive?

15 If the exchange rate is 1 CAD = 0.56 JOD, how much JOD would you receive for 500 CAD?

16 Ali traveled from the UAE to London and exchanged 2,500 AED to GBP. If he received 500 GBP, how much was 1 AED worth in GBP?

17 Michael wants to travel to South Africa and exchange USD $800. If the exchange rate is 1 USD = 16.50 South African rand (ZAR), how much will Michael receive in ZAR?

18 Emily is traveling from Canada to Jordan and wants to exchange 2,500 CAD to JOD. If the exchange rate is 1 CAD = 0.55 JOD, how much JOD will Emily receive?

19 John is visiting Dubai from the UK and wants to convert 600 GBP to AED. If the exchange rate is 1 GBP = 5.10 AED, how much AED will John receive?

20 Maria is traveling from Germany to Australia and wants to exchange 1,000 euros (EUR) to Australian dollars (AUD). If the exchange rate is 1 EUR = 1.50 AUD, how much AUD will Maria receive?

21 Liam traveled from Australia to France and exchanged 2,500 AUD to euros. If he received 1,750 EUR, how much was 1 AUD worth in EUR?

22 Emma wants to buy a designer handbag in Paris for 600 EUR. If the exchange rate is 1 EUR = 1.20 AUD, how much will Emma pay in AUD?

23 Sarah is traveling from Australia to Italy and converted 5,000 AUD to EUR. If she received 3,200 EUR, how much was 1 AUD worth in EUR?

24 Olivia is visiting Sydney from Spain and wants to convert 800 EUR to AUD. If the exchange rate is 1 EUR = 1.40 AUD, how much AUD will Olivia receive?

25 Juan is traveling from Argentina to Brazil and wants to exchange 2,000 Argentine pesos (ARS) to Brazilian reals (BRL). If the exchange rate is 1 ARS = 0.06 BRL, how many BRL will Juan receive?

26 Sofia is visiting Peru from Colombia and wants to convert 1,500 Colombian pesos (COP) to Peruvian soles (PEN). If the exchange rate is 1 COP = 0.003 PEN, how many PEN will Sofia receive?

27 Carlos is traveling from Chile to Argentina and wants to exchange 100,000 Chilean pesos (CLP) to ARS. If the exchange rate is 1 CLP = 0.09 ARS, how many ARS will Carlos receive?

28 Ana wants to buy souvenirs in Uruguay and needs to convert 500 BRL to Uruguayan pesos (UYU). If the exchange rate is 1 BRL = 8.50 UYU, how many UYU will Ana receive?

29 Diego is traveling from Peru to Bolivia and wants to exchange 1,000 PEN to Bolivian bolivianos (BOB). If the exchange rate is 1 PEN = 0.60 BOB, how many BOB will Diego receive?

30 Hiroshi is traveling from Japan to the United States and wants to exchange 100,000 Japanese yen (JPY) to USD. If the exchange rate is 1 USD = 110 JPY, how many USD will Hiroshi receive?

31 Emi wants to buy a camera in Japan for 50,000 JPY. If the exchange rate is 1 USD = 112 JPY, how much will Emi pay in USD?

32 Takashi exchanged 1,000 USD to JPY and received 111,000 JPY. What was the exchange rate?

33 Yuki is traveling from Japan to Australia and wants to convert 200,000 JPY to AUD. If the exchange rate is 1 AUD = 85 JPY, how many AUD will Yuki receive?

34 Raj is traveling from India to the United Kingdom and wants to exchange 50,000 Indian rupees (INR) to GBP. If the exchange rate is 1 GBP = 100 INR, how many GBP will Raj receive?

35 Priya wants to buy a saree in India for 5,000 rupees. If the exchange rate is 1 USD = 75 INR, how much will Priya pay in USD?

36 Sanjay exchanged 1,000 USD to rupees and received 75,000 INR. What was the exchange rate?

37 Neeta is traveling from India to Canada and wants to convert 10,000 INR to Canadian dollars (CAD). If the exchange rate is 1 CAD = 55 INR, how many CAD will Neeta receive?

38 Sarah purchases an NFT for 0.05 Ethereum (ETH). If the exchange rate is 1 ETH = $2,500, what is the cost of the NFT in USD?

39 David buys an NFT for 0.1 Bitcoin (BTC). If the current Bitcoin price is $40,000 per BTC, what is the cost of the NFT in USD?

40 Emily purchases an NFT for 800 EUR. If the current exchange rate is 1 EUR = 1.15 USD, what is the cost of the NFT in USD?

2.7 Renting v. Buying

Deciding whether to rent or purchase a property or a car is a major decision that will require you to carefully evaluate various factors. Here are some key considerations you should keep in mind when deciding between buying and renting.

Financial Considerations

● Affordability: Assess your financial situation, including upfront costs, ongoing payments, insurance, taxes, maintenance expenses and employment/income stability. Determine if purchasing fits within your budget or if renting offers a more manageable financial arrangement.

- Long-term Costs: Consider the overall costs of ownership, including depreciation, interest rates, repairs, and potential resale value. Compare these costs with the fixed rental payments and potential rental rate increases.

Practical Considerations

- Usage and Duration: Evaluate your intended usage and the expected duration of ownership or rental. If you need long-term, consistent access, purchasing may be beneficial. Conversely, if your needs are temporary or sporadic, renting might be a more suitable option.

- Flexibility: Assess the level of flexibility required. Renting provides the advantage of easily changing or upgrading to suit evolving needs, while ownership offers stability and customization options.

Personal Preferences and Lifestyle

- Customization: Consider the importance of personalizing the item to your preferences. Ownership allows for customization, whether it's modifying a home or vehicle, whereas renting may have restrictions.

- Responsibilities: Reflect on the responsibilities associated with ownership, such as maintenance, repairs, and managing property or vehicle-related tasks. Renting typically relieves individuals of these responsibilities, offering a hassle-free experience.

Future Considerations

- Investment Potential: Weigh the potential investment value and future financial returns. Purchasing property or a vehicle may offer the opportunity for equity or appreciation, while renting offers flexibility but no ownership benefits (unless it is a rent-to-own type of contract).

- Life Changes: Anticipate circumstances such as a job relocation, change in employment status or even a lifestyle adjustment when starting a family. Assess how these factors might impact your decision and whether owning or renting can accommodate these changes effectively.

Analyzing these factors will help you make a well-informed choice that aligns with your current circumstances, long-term goals, and desired lifestyle. Remember, there is no one-size-fits-all answer, and the best decision will ultimately depend on individual circumstances and priorities.

Now, let's try the following questions.

1 Adam is deciding between purchasing a car for $25,000 or renting a car for $400 per month. If he plans to keep the car for 5 years, which option costs less (based solely on the information provided)?

2 Jessica is deciding between purchasing a used textbook for $60 or renting it for $1.20 per week. If she needs the textbook for 52 weeks, which option costs less?

3 Isabella is deciding between purchasing a dress for $79.99 or renting it for $13.50 per occasion. If she plans to wear the dress 6 times, which option is more financially sensible?

4 John is considering purchasing a smartphone for $800 or renting it for $40 per month. If he plans to use the phone for 2 years, which option is more cost-effective, based solely on this information?

5 Sarah is deciding between purchasing a power tool for $200 or renting it for $15 per day. If she needs the tool for 10 days only, which option is more financially sensible?

6   Buy or Lease a Car?

Monthly lease payment: $300
Lease term: 48 months
Lease cost: $300 x 48 = $14,400

Car purchase price: $25,000
Down payment: $5,000
Loan Amount: $25,000 - $5,000 = $20,000
Loan term: 48 months
Interest rate: 5%

Think about the pros and cons of buying or leasing a car in this scenario.

7   Buy or Lease Property?

Monthly rent: $1,500
Lease term: 12 months
Total lease cost: $1,500 x 12 = $18,000

Property purchase price: $300,000
Down payment: $60,000
Loan Amount: $300,000 - $60,000 = $240,000
Loan term: 30 years
Interest rate: 4%

Think about pros and cons of buying or leasing a property in this scenario.

UNIT 3

Budgeting

Learning how to budget is crucial as it equips you with essential financial skills that are relevant throughout your life. Here are some key reasons why it is important to learn how to budget:

- **Financial Responsibility and Independence:** Budgeting helps you understand the value of money, the importance of saving, and the consequences of overspending. By learning to live within your means and prioritize spending, you can avoid relying on others for financial support.

- **Goal Setting and Planning:** Whether you are saving for college, purchasing a car or planning a trip, budgeting helps you prioritize your spending and allocate funds towards your goals.

- **Debt Avoidance**: Budgeting helps you avoid excessive debt and establish a healthy credit history and maintain financial independence.

- **Building a Savings Habit and Financial Preparedness:** Budgeting encourages you to develop a savings habit and set aside money for emergencies and responsibilities that lie ahead such as education, rent, utilities and other financial obligations.

3.1 Multiple Purchases and Budgeting

Let's try some questions budgeting questions.

1   Mariam wants to buy a dress for $45, a handbag for $30, and a pair of earrings for $20. If she has $100, will she have enough money to buy all three items?

2   Ahmed wants to purchase a laptop for $800, a printer originally priced at $120 using a coupon of 15% off, and a mouse originally priced at $30 at a discount of 10%. If he has $900, will he have enough money to buy all three items?

3   Alia wants to buy a sweater for $25, a scarf for $15, and a pair of gloves for $10. If there is a sale of 17% off on all the items and she has $40, will she have enough money to buy all three items?

4   Diala wants to buy a bike for $250 and a helmet for $40. If they are discounted at 25% off and she has $200, will she have enough money to buy both items?

5   Abdullah wants to purchase a concert ticket that costs $100, plus 1% tax and a shipping fee of $15. He currently has $50. How much more money does he need to save to afford the ticket?

6   Samir receives $400 for his birthday. He decides to spend 40% of it on a concert ticket, save 30%, and donate 10%. How much money will he have leftover to buy anything else?

7   You have $1,000 in your bank account. Your monthly expenses include $400 for rent, $200 for groceries, $100 for utilities, and $150 for transportation. Will you have sufficient funds to purchase a concert ticket for $149?

8   You have $300 and want to buy a new phone that costs $250, plus 12% tax. However, you also need to save at least $25. Can you afford to buy the phone and still meet your savings goal?

9   Maria receives $500 as a gift. She decides to allocate 30% to savings, 40% to spending, and the rest to donating. How much money will she allocate to each category?

10 You have $1,000 to spend on a vacation. You want to spend 40% on accommodation, 25% on transportation, and the rest on activities. How much money will you allocate to each category?

11 Isabelle has $600 to spend on groceries, dining out, and entertainment. She wants to allocate 50% to groceries, 30% to dining out, and the rest to entertainment. How much money will she allocate to each category?

12 You have $800 and want to spend it on clothes, shoes, and accessories. You want to spend 60% on clothes, 25% on shoes, and the rest on accessories. How much money will you allocate to each category?

13 You receive $400 from a part-time job. You want to allocate 30% to savings, 40% to spending, and the rest to charity. How much money will you allocate to each category?

14 Byungoon has $1,200 in his bank account. He wants to spend 20% on clothes, 30% on electronics, and the rest on books. How much money will he allocate to each category?

15 You have $500 and want to allocate it toward saving for a concert ticket, buying a new phone, and going out with friends. You decide to save 40% for the concert ticket, spend 30% on the phone, and the rest on going out. How much money will you allocate to each category?

16 You have $1,000 and want to allocate it toward buying a new computer, saving for a car, and donating to charity. You decide to spend $780 on the computer, save 10% for the car, and the rest on donations. How much money will you allocate to donations?

17 John receives a monthly allowance of $500 while in college. He needs to allocate his allowance towards buying books, meals, entertainment, and other monthly expenses. He wants to spend 30% of his allowance on books, 40% on meals, 20% on entertainment, and the remaining amount on other expenses. How much money should he allocate for each category?

18 Emily has a monthly allowance of $700 while in college. She wants to allocate 35% for meals, 20% for entertainment, and the rest equally between books and other expenses. How much money should she allocate for each category?

19 Sajida has a monthly income of $1,500. She wants to budget her expenses and has identified necessary items such as rent ($500), food ($300), and utilities ($150). She also wants to allocate some money for entertainment and clothes shopping. If she wants to save at least $200 per month, how much should she limit her budget for entertainment and clothes shopping?

20 David spends $30 per week on eating at restaurants. If he limits his restaurant expenses to $15 per week, how much money can he save in one year?

21 Sophie has a monthly income of $1,200. She needs to budget for rent ($500), utilities ($100), groceries ($200), and transportation ($100). She also wants to allocate money for entertainment and hobbies. How much should Sophie budget for entertainment and hobbies if she wants to save at least 20% of her income per month?

22 Alex has a monthly income of $2,000. He has monthly expenses of $1,500, including rent, utilities, and food. How much money can Alex save in a year if he allocates 20% of his income towards savings?

23 David is on a tight budget and needs to plan his grocery shopping for the week. He wants to allocate 30% of his weekly income to groceries. If David earns $500 per week, how much should he allocate for grocery shopping per month?

24 Dana wants to create a budget for her grocery shopping. She has a list of items she needs to buy, along with their prices. If Dana wants to stick to a budget of $20 per week, can she afford all the items on her list?

  A   Milk: $2.50
  B   Bread: $3.00
  C   Eggs: $2.20
  D   Chicken: $8.50
  E   Vegetables: $4.00

3.2 50/30/20 Rule

The 50/30/20 budgeting rule is a popular method of allocating your income to different categories in order to achieve a balanced financial plan. It suggests dividing your after-tax income into three broad categories: needs, wants, and savings/debt repayment. Here's a detailed breakdown of each category:

Needs (50% of your budget): This category includes essential expenses that are necessary for your day-to day living. It typically encompasses fixed costs that are relatively inflexible and must be paid regularly. Here are some examples of needs:

A   Housing: This includes rent or mortgage payments, property taxes, and homeowners' or renters' insurance.

B   Utilities: Expenses like electricity, water, heating, and internet bills.

C   Transportation: Monthly car loan payments, fuel costs, insurance, and maintenance expenses.

D   Groceries: The amount you spend on food and essential household supplies.

E   Health care: Health insurance premiums, prescription medications, and medical bills.

F   Minimum debt payments: The required payments for any outstanding loans or credit card debts.

Ideally, you should aim to allocate around 50% of your after-tax income toward meeting these essential needs.

Wants (30% of your budget): This category includes discretionary expenses that enhance your lifestyle but aren't vital for survival. These are expenses that you have some control over and can adjust as needed. Examples of wants include:

A   Dining out: Eating at restaurants, ordering takeout, or enjoying social outings.

B   Entertainment: Movies, concerts, streaming services, hobbies, and vacations.

C   Shopping: Non-essential clothing, electronics, gadgets and other personal items.

D   Subscriptions: Magazine subscriptions, gym memberships, or other non-essential services.

E   Travel: Weekend getaways, family vacations or exploring new destinations.

It is recommended to allocate around 30% of your after-tax income for these discretionary expenses.

Savings and Debt Repayment (20% of your budget): This category focuses on securing your financial future and managing existing debts. It includes saving for emergencies, retirement, and paying down debts faster. Here is what you can allocate within this category:

A   Emergency fund: Building and maintaining a fund to cover unexpected expenses or job loss.

B   Retirement savings: Contributing to retirement accounts or pension plans.

C   Debt repayment: Accelerating payments towards loans, credit card debt or student loans.

D   Long-term savings: Investing in stocks, mutual funds, real estate or other long-term goals.

It is advisable to allocate at least 20% of your after-tax income toward savings and debt repayment to foster financial stability and work towards your future goals.

Remember, the 50/30/20 budgeting rule serves as a general guideline. Depending on your unique circumstances and financial goals, you can adjust the percentages to better suit your needs. Regularly reviewing and adjusting your budget is crucial to maintaining financial balance and adapting to changing circumstances.

Let's try these questions to see how the 50/30/20 rule works.

1   John's after-tax monthly income is $3,000. Apply the 50/30/20 rule to determine how much he should allocate to each category (needs, wants and savings & debt repayment).

2   Mary earns a monthly after-tax income of $5,000. Apply the 50/30/20 rule to determine the amounts for each category (needs, wants and savings & debt repayment).

3   Sara's after-tax monthly income is $2,500. Apply the 50/30/20 rule to determine how much she should allocate to each category (needs, wants and savings & debt repayment).

4   Tom's after-tax monthly income is $4,500. If he wants to spend $1,750 on a beach holiday in Hawaii, will he be within the limits of the 50/30/20 rule?

5   Nafisa's after-tax monthly income is $6,000. If Nafisa requires braces that will cost her $2,500, will she be able to pay for the braces within the 50/30/20 rule?

6   Place the following items into the Needs, Wants or Savings/Debt Repayment categories: Rent, groceries, dining out, Netflix subscription, retirement fund, new iphone 13.

7   Place the following items into the Needs, Wants or Savings/Debt Repayment categories: Health insurance, movie tickets, emergency fund, gym membership, vacation savings, utility bills.

Let's Explore

8   You've been diligently following the 50/30/20 rule to manage your finances. Your monthly income is $3,000. As part of this rule, you allocate $1,500 (50%) to cover your needs, $900 (30%) for your wants, and $600 (20%) for savings and debt repayment. You've planned to purchase a new gadget for $300 and go on a weekend getaway with your friends for $600, both of which fall within your "wants" category. Suddenly, you're faced with an unexpected car repair bill of $800 and have already used up funds from the "needs" category.

   A   How might this unexpected expense impact your original plans to purchase the gadget and go on vacation?

   B   What factors should you consider when deciding whether to use your "wants" money for the car repair or to continue with your original plans?

   C   How can having an emergency fund in place help you make these decisions more confidently and responsibly?

UNIT 4

Shared Costs

Sharing costs with friends can be a convenient and cost-effective way to manage expenses. However, it is essential to be aware of your obligations and liabilities in these situations. To avoid misunderstandings and conflict, you should consider the following when sharing costs:

A   Before agreeing to share expenses, you should communicate openly and clearly about how costs will be divided and clarify each person's share.

B   Understand that sharing expenses means sharing responsibilities for payment. For example, if some of your friends leave a restaurant without paying their portion, you may be held responsible for the entire bill. The restaurant expects payment for the services provided, and as a customer, you have the responsibility to settle the bill.

C   Be aware of legal implications. In some cases, shared expenses may have legal implications. For example, renting an apartment together may involve signing a lease agreement, making all tenants jointly responsible for rent and damages. Signing a rental agreement with others means that if they fail to pay their share or delay payments, you may still be legally responsible for the full rent and may face potential financial and legal consequences, including additional charges for late payments imposed by the landlord or property management.

D   Avoid late penalty charges or other negative legal or financial consequences by ensuring that payments for shared spaces are made in a timely manner.

4.1 Dividing the Bill and Tip

1   You and two friends go out for dinner. The bill is $90, and you want to leave a 15% tip. How much does each person need to pay?

2   You and four friends have lunch. The bill is $120, and you want to leave a 20% tip. How much does each person need to pay?

3 You and three friends go out for a meal. The bill is $75, and you want to leave a 18% tip. How much does each person need to pay?

4 You and five friends have dinner. The bill is $200, and you want to leave a 15% tip. How much does each person need to pay?

5 You and three friends go out for dinner, and the bill comes to $120. You decide to split the bill and offer to pay 50% while the other three share the remaining 50% equally. How much does each person have to pay?

6 You and four friends dine at a restaurant and receive a bill of $200 in total. You want to split the bill, with everyone contributing equally, but your portion will be an additional $20. How much does each person have to pay?

7 You and five friends go out for a celebratory dinner, and the bill comes to $300. However, one friend is unable to contribute. How much does each person have to pay to cover the bill?

8 You and four friends go out for lunch, and the bill comes to $80. You decide to split the bill equally, but one friend realizes they only have enough money to pay for half of their portion of the bill. How much does each person have to pay to cover the bill?

9 You and four friends go out for dinner, and the bill comes to $150. You decide to split the bill based on each person's order. Person A's order was $30, Person B's order was $25, Person C's order was $35, Person D's order was $20, and Person E's order was $40. What percentage of the bill does each person pay?

4.2 Dividing the Rent

When signing a rental lease, especially with roommates, there are several important factors to be aware of. Here is a summary of key considerations:

- Understand the Lease Terms: Read the lease thoroughly and understand all the terms and conditions. Pay attention to details such as the lease duration, rent amount, security deposit, late payment penalties, maintenance responsibilities, pet policies, and any restrictions or rules specific to the property.

- Joint and Several Liability: Be aware that most leases hold all tenants jointly and severally liable. This means that each roommate is individually responsible for the full rent payment and any damages or lease violations, regardless of the contributions or actions of other roommates.

- Rental Payment Arrangements: Discuss and agree upon the rental payment arrangements with your roommates. Determine how the rent will be divided among roommates, who will be responsible for submitting the payment to the landlord, and establish a plan for handling any late or missed payments.

- Security Deposit: Understand the security deposit requirements and ensure that it is clearly documented how the deposit will be divided among roommates at the end of the lease. Consider creating an inventory checklist and taking photos of the rental unit's condition to avoid disputes when reclaiming the deposit.

- Roommate Agreement: Consider drafting a roommate agreement that outlines shared responsibilities, such as chores, utilities, visitor policies, quiet hours, and any other expectations to maintain a harmonious living environment. This agreement can help address potential conflicts and provide clarity on roommate-specific matters.

- Subletting and Lease Termination: Review the lease provisions regarding subletting and early termination. Determine the procedures and requirements for adding or removing roommates from the lease, as well as the potential financial implications.

- Communication and Conflict Resolution: Establish open lines of communication with your roommates to address any issues or concerns promptly. Encourage respectful dialogue and establish a process for conflict resolution to maintain a positive living environment.

- Documentation: Keep copies of the signed lease agreement, rent payment receipts and any written communication related to the rental. These documents can serve as evidence in case of disputes or misunderstandings.

- Legal Advice: If you have any concerns or uncertainties regarding the lease agreement, it is advisable to seek legal advice. A lawyer experienced in real estate or tenant law can review the lease and provide guidance specific to your situation.

By being aware of these considerations and addressing them proactively, you can help ensure a smooth and mutually beneficial living arrangement with your roommates while minimizing the potential for conflicts or misunderstandings.

Think about these concepts as you work through the following problems.

1   You and three roommates share an apartment with a monthly rent of $2,800. You agree to pay 60% of the rent, while the other three share the remaining 40% equally. How much does each person need to pay?

2   You and two friends decide to rent a beach house for a week, costing $3,500 in total. You want to split the cost proportionally based on each person's income, relative to the total income of all three friends. Your income is $40,000, Friend A's income is $50,000, and Friend B's income is $60,000. How much does each person have to contribute?

3   You, Malika and Shinaya decide to split the rent for a three-bedroom apartment. The total monthly rent is $2,400. You decide to take the master bedroom, which costs $900 per month. Malika takes bedroom A (75% of remaining rent, and Shinaya takes bedroom B (25% of remaining rent). How much does each person need to pay towards rent?

4   You and three friends decide to rent a vacation home for six days. The total cost is $2,700. However, one friend can only stay for the first three days. How much does each person have to pay to cover the cost?

5   You and three friends rent a four bedroom beach house for a weekend, costing $1,200. You and Ibrahim agree to pay 60% of the rent, while Amjad and Mike will share the remaining rent equally. There is an additional $75 electricity charge that will also be shared based on room consumption. Your room consumes 32% of the electricity bill, while the other rooms combined consume 68%. How much does each person have to pay in rent and electricity?

6   You and two roommates rent an apartment for $2,400 per month. Karima pays 40% of the rent, while you and Amari split the remaining 60% equally. How much does each person need to pay?

7   You, Mary and Joe rent a vacation house for $2,050 per week. You and Mary will remain for the entire week, while Joe will only stay for the first three days and does not want to pay for the entire week. How much should each person pay?

8   You and three roommates decide to divide the monthly rent of $1,800 based on the square footage of each room. The total square footage of the apartment is 2,000 square feet. Your room is 600 square feet, Roommate A's room is 500 square feet, Roommate B's room is 400 square feet, and Roommate C's room is 500 square feet. How much does each person need to contribute?

9   Rushabh, Arman and Isht decide to evenly split the monthly rent of $2,500, but Isht will join the lease and move in after two months. How much does each person need to contribute for the first two months?

10 Rubin, Messi and Ronaldo decide to divide the monthly utility bills based on usage. Rubin's room consumes 47% of the electrical charges and 19% of the internet charges. If this month's electricity bill is $150 and the internet bill is $98, how much will Rubin pay towards utility bills?

11 You, Mariam, Fatima and Julie decide to split the monthly utility bill of $240 equally. However, Julie will be away for two weeks and wants to only pay for the time that she spends at the apartment. How much does each person need to contribute?

12 You and your roommates decide to split the monthly water bill of $80 based on the number of people in each room. Your room has one person, Roommate A's room has two people, Roommate B's room has three people, Roommate C's room has two people, and Roommate D's room has one person. How much does each room need to contribute?

13 You, Ajesh and Kumar decide to divide the monthly electricity bill of $120 equally. However, Kumar will be away for a week and wants to pay a reduced amount. How much does each person need to contribute?

14 You and seven roommates decide to split the monthly internet bill of $90 based on the number of people in each room. Your room has two people, Roommate A's room has one person, Roommate B's room has three people, and Roommate C's room has two people. How much does each room need to contribute?

15 You, Brigitte, Isabelle and Florence decide to sign a nine-month lease for $9,360 to be split equally. However, Florence will only be staying for the first eight months and wants to pay a reduced amount. How much does each person need to contribute in total for the duration of the lease?

16 You and three roommates decide to split the monthly gas bill of $80 based on the square footage of each room. The total square footage of the apartment is 1,200 square feet. Your room is 400 square feet, Roommate A's room is 300 square feet, Roommate B's room is 200 square feet, and Roommate C's room is 300 square feet. How much does each room need to contribute?

17 You and your two roommates decide to rent a two-bedroom apartment and split the monthly rent and utilities based on room type, with single rooms paying 50% in rent and utilities. Your room is a single room and the other room is a double room. The monthly rent is $960 and the monthly utility bills are $140. How much does each person pay in monthly rent and utilities?

18 Madonna, Kylie, Kim and Chloe decide to divide the monthly internet bill of $90 equally. However, Chloe will only be staying for one week and wants to pay a reduced amount. How much does each person need to contribute?

19 Imagine you're planning to rent an apartment with two roommates. The monthly rent for the apartment is $1,500. The landlord requires a security deposit equal to one month's rent, and the first and last month's rent upfront. Each roommate will be added to the lease. Here is the scenario:

- You and your roommates will equally split the rent.

- Each of you will be responsible for paying one-third of the rent each month.

- The security deposit and first/last month's rent will be split equally among you.

Now let's consider the following situations:

A   What financial challenges might arise if one of your roommates doesn't pay their share of the rent or decides to move out unexpectedly?

B   If one of your roommates causes significant damage to the apartment, how might this impact the security deposit and the relationship among your roommates?

C   What proactive steps can you take to address these potential issues and ensure a smooth co-living experience among your roommates?

UNIT 5

Taxes

Welcome to the Taxes section, where we will delve into the world of taxes and learn how to calculate them. Taxes are mandatory financial contributions imposed by governments on individuals and businesses to fund public services, infrastructure and government operations such as education, healthcare and public transportation. Taxes can vary depending on factors such as income level, applicable tax laws and whether the individual or entity is considered a resident or non-resident for tax purposes.

Let's take a closer look at the different types of taxes. (Please note that tax rates can vary depending on various factors such as income level, jurisdiction and tax laws. The rates used in this unit are fictional and provided for educational purposes).

5.1 Sales Tax

Sales tax is a consumption-based tax that generates revenue for government programs and services. It is usually charged as a percentage of the purchase price at the point of sale and collected by the retailer, who then remits it to the government. The specific rate of sales tax can vary depending on the jurisdiction and the type of goods or services being sold.

Let's try some sales tax questions.

1   A shirt costs $25 before tax. If the tax rate is 7%, what is the total cost of the shirt including tax?

2   A laptop is priced at $800 before tax. If the tax rate is 9%, what is the total cost of the laptop including tax?

3   A pair of shoes costs $65 before tax. If the tax rate is 6%, what is the total cost of the shoes including tax?

4   A book costs $15 before tax. If the tax rate is 8%, what is the total cost of the book including tax?

5   A jacket costs $120 before tax. If the tax rate is 10%, what is the total cost of the jacket including tax?

6 A restaurant bill comes to $45 before tax. If the tax rate is 8%, what is the total cost of the bill including tax?

7 A group dines at a restaurant with a bill of $92.65, including tax. If the tax rate is 9%, what is the total cost of the bill excluding tax?

8 A meal at a restaurant costs $32.10, including tax. If the tax rate is 7%, what is the total cost of the meal excluding tax?

9 Reneigh purchases a t-shirt and the receipt total is $53.25 including sales tax of 6.5%. What is the price of the t-shirt before tax?

10 An item is priced at $120, and the sales tax rate is 7.5%. What is the amount paid in tax?

11 An item is priced at $65, and the sales tax rate is 9.5%. What is the amount of tax paid?

5.2 Tax and Gratuity

In many countries it is customary practice to show gratitude for good service by paying a gratuity or tip. The amount of gratuity is usually based on a percentage of the bill or the level of satisfaction with the service provided. Pay attention to your bill because in some establishments, the gratuity is automatically included in the bill and will normally appear as a separate charge in the itemized list on the bill. If it does not appear on the bill, then it is usually left to the discretion of the customer to decide whether and how much to leave as a gratuity.

Try the following problems.

1 You have a dinner bill of $45 before tax and tip. The tax rate is 7% and you want to leave a 15% tip on the amount after tax. Calculate the total cost of the bill, including tax and tip.

2 You purchase a cake for $35 before tax and tip. The tax rate is 8% and you want to leave a 20% tip on the amount before tax. Determine the total cost of the cake including tax and tip.

3   You have a bill at a restaurant of $75 before tax and tip. The tax rate is 7% and you want to leave a 18% tip on the amount before tax. Find the total cost of the bill, including tax and tip.

4   You order a dessert for $8 before tax and tip. The tax rate is 9% and you want to leave a 20% tip on the amount after tax. Determine the total cost of the dessert, including tax and tip.

5   You have a bill at a café of $50 before tax and tip. The tax rate is 8% and you want to leave a 15% tip on the amount before tax. Find the total cost of the bill, including tax and tip.

6   Your total bill at a restaurant is $120. The tax rate is 6% and you want to leave a 22% tip on the amount before tax. What is the total amount you will pay?

7   You have a dinner bill of $137.33 including 8% tax and 15% tip (on amount before tax). (a) What is the amount of the tax and tip paid? (b) What is the amount of the bill before tax and tip?

5.3 Income Tax

In this section, we will explore the implications of income tax, which can be imposed at different rates according to the tax laws of different jurisdictions and countries. Income tax is typically calculated based on the individual's or business's taxable income. The tax rate varies depending on the income level and the tax brackets set by a government. Understanding income tax is crucial for financial literacy as it helps individuals and businesses plan their finances, budget effectively and meet their tax obligations.

Let's try some income tax questions.

1   In your country, the income tax rates are as follows: 10% for the first $10,000, 15% for the next $10,000, and 20% for any income above $20,000. If a person earns $25,000, what is their income tax liability?

2 Using the tax rates from the preceding question, what is the income tax liability for a person earning $15,000?

3 In Urdovia, the income tax rates are as follows: 5% for the first $8,000, 10% for the next $12,000, and 15% for any income above $20,000. If a person earns $25,000, what is their income tax liability?

4 Using the tax rates from the preceding question, what is the income tax liability for a person earning $10,000?

5 In Mathnasia, the income tax rates are as follows: 15% for the first $20,000, 25% for the next $30,000, and 30% for any income above $50,000. If a person earns $60,000, what is their income tax liability?

6 Using the tax rates from the preceding question, what is the income tax liability for a person earning $15,000?

7 In Finance Island, the income tax rates are as follows: 20% for the first $15,000, 30% for the next $25,000, and 35% for any income above $40,000. If a person earns $50,000, what is their income tax liability?

8 Using the tax rates from the preceding question, what is the income tax liability for a person earning $10,000?

9 In Numbers Island, the income tax rates are as follows: 10% for the first $10,000, 20% for the next $15,000, and 25% for any income above $25,000. If a person earns $30,000, what is their income tax liability?

10 Josh lives in Taxasia, where he earns $118,000 a year and pays 12.5% income tax. The income tax return filing deadline is December 31 of each year. Josh misses the deadline and has to pay a 2% penalty fee on the tax owed. (a) How much income tax does Josh owe (b) What is the amount of the penalty fee he must pay?

11 In the Isles of Finance, the income tax rates are as follows: 10% for the first $15,000, 15% for the next $20,000, and 20% for any income above $35,000. If a person earns $30,000, what is their income tax liability?

12 Using the tax rates from the preceding question, what is the income tax liability for a person earning $10,000?

13 In the United States of Finance, the income tax rates are as follows: 10% for the first $25,000, 15% for the next $30,000, and 20% for any income above $55,000. If a person earns $60,000, what is their income tax liability?

14 Samia lives in Financia, where is must pay 17% tax on the $250,000 she earns per year. She misses the income tax return filing deadline and therefore, has to pay a 5% penalty on the amount of income tax owed. (a) How much income tax does she owe? (b) What is the amount of the penalty fee she must pay?

5.4 Investment Tax

Tax on investments refers to the taxes imposed on the income or gains generated from investments such as stocks, bonds, real estate and other financial instruments. This can include capital gains tax, dividend tax, interest income tax, rental income tax and other applicable taxes depending on the specific investment and the tax regulations of the country.

a. Capital Gains Tax

Please note that these calculations assume that the entire gain is subject to capital gains tax and do not account for any deductions, exemptions, or other factors that may affect the actual tax liability, unless specifically stated.

1 John purchased a stock for $1,000 and later sold it for $1,500. If the capital gains tax rate is 20%, how much capital gains tax will John owe?

2   Sarah sold a piece of artwork for $10,000. She initially purchased it for $8,000. If the capital gains tax rate is 15%, how much capital gains tax will Sarah owe?

3   Mark inherited a property with a fair market value of $200,000. He sold it for $250,000. If the capital gains tax rate is 25%, how much capital gains tax will Mark owe?

4   Emily bought shares in a mutual fund for $5,000 and later sold them for $7,500. If the capital gains tax rate is 10%, how much capital gains tax will Emily owe?

5   Michael purchased a rental property for $150,000 and sold it for $200,000. If the capital gains tax rate is 30%, how much capital gains tax will Michael owe?

b. Dividend Tax

Please note that dividend tax rates can vary based on various factors such as income level, jurisdiction, and tax laws. The rates used in these questions are fictional and provided for educational purposes.

1   Sarah received $1,500 in dividends from her stock investments. If the dividend tax rate is 15%, how much dividend tax will Sarah owe?

2   Mark earned $2,000 in dividends from his mutual fund investments. If the dividend tax rate is 20%, how much dividend tax will Mark owe?

3   Emily received $500 in dividends from her savings account. If the dividend tax rate is 10%, how much dividend tax will Emily owe?

4   Michael earned $5,000 in dividends from his stock portfolio. If the dividend tax rate is 25%, how much dividend tax will Michael owe?

5   David received $10,000 in dividends from his investments. If the dividend tax rate is 30%, how much dividend tax will David owe?

c. Interest Income Tax

Please note that interest income tax rates can vary based on various factors such as income level, jurisdiction, and tax laws. The rates used in these questions are fictional and provided for educational purposes.

1   Sarah earned $500 in interest income from her savings account. If the interest income tax rate is 10%, how much interest income tax will Sarah owe?

2   Emily earned $200 in interest income from her bond investments. If the interest income tax rate is 20%, how much interest income tax will Emily owe?

3   Michael received $2,500 in interest income from his corporate bonds. If the interest income tax rate is 25%, how much interest income tax will Michael owe?

4   David earned $5,000 in interest income from his savings accounts and certificates of deposit. If the interest income tax rate is 30%, how much interest income tax will David owe?

d. Rental Income Tax

Please note that rental income tax rates can vary based on various factors such as income level, jurisdiction and tax laws. The rates used in these questions are fictional and provided for educational purposes.

1   Sarah rented out her apartment and earned $1,200 per month in rental income. If the rental income tax rate is 20%, how much rental income tax will Sarah owe for the year?

2   Mark owns a rental property and receives $2,500 per month in rental income. If the rental income tax rate is 15%, how much rental income tax will Mark owe for the year?

3   Emily is a citizen and resident of Taxnation, where she earns $800 per week in rental income. (a) If the rental income tax rate is 25%, how much rental income tax will Emily owe for the year? If Emily relocates to Mathnation she is considered

to be a non-resident of Taxnation and must now pay 30% tax on this rental income. (b) What is the amount of rental income tax she must pay as a non-resident of Taxnation?

4 David lives in Ice Nation, where he rents out his commercial property for $5,000 per month. (a) If the rental income tax rate is 35%, how much rental income tax will David owe for the year? If David relocates to Sunshine Nation, he will be considered to be a non-resident of Ice Nation and taxed at a rate of 45% on the rental income from his commercial property. (b) What is the amount of tax he will owe as a non-resident of Ice Nation?

5.5 Property Tax

Property tax is a form of taxation imposed by some local governments on property owners, and usually serves as a significant source of revenue that funds essential public services such as schools, infrastructure, public safety, and local administration. Property tax rates and regulations can vary widely depending on the location and jurisdiction, but the fundamental concept remains consistent: property owners are required to pay a certain percentage of their property's assessed value as tax.

Some key points about property tax include:

● Assessed Value: The property tax is typically based on the assessed value of the property. This value is determined by local assessors and reflects an estimate of the property's market value. The assessment process may consider factors like property size, location, improvements and comparable sales.

● Tax Rates: Property tax rates are expressed as a percentage of the assessed value. These rates vary from one locality to another and can be influenced by factors such as budgetary needs, public services, and economic conditions. Rates are often set by local governments, including municipalities, counties and school districts.

- Tax Calculation: To calculate property tax, the assessed value of the property is multiplied by the applicable tax rate. This results in the annual property tax liability. Different jurisdictions might have various exemptions, deductions and caps that can influence the final tax amount.

- Progressive and Regressive Taxation: Property tax systems can be progressive or regressive. Progressive systems involve higher tax rates for higher property values, whereas regressive systems apply uniform rates regardless of property value. Some jurisdictions also offer tax relief measures, such as homestead exemptions or senior citizen discounts, to ease the burden on certain property owners.

Let's try some property tax questions.

1 John owns a property with an assessed value of $250,000. The local property tax rate is 1.2%. Calculate the annual property tax John needs to pay.

2 Sarah's house is assessed at $400,000. The property tax rate is 0.8%. However, homeowners are eligible for a 20% tax exemption. Calculate the annual property tax she needs to pay after the exemption.

3 Alex's property has an assessed value of $180,000. The local property tax rate is 2.5%. However, there is a fixed deduction of $2,000 from the assessed value before applying the tax rate. Calculate the annual property tax.

4 Emily's property has an assessed value of $300,000. The property tax rate is 1.5%, and there's an additional local school tax rate of 0.7%. Calculate the total annual property tax including the school tax.

5 David's property is subject to a progressive property tax rate based on assessed value:

   - For the first $150,000, the tax rate is 1.0%.

   - For the portion above $150,000, the tax rate is 1.5%.

If the assessed value of David's property is $220,000, calculate the annual property tax.

5.6 Inheritance Tax

Inheritance tax is typically calculated based on the value of the inherited asset. Countries have different inheritance tax laws and requirements governing how assets are taxed and transferred upon death of an individual, including the applicable tax rates, exemptions and filing obligations.

Please note that inheritance tax rates can vary based on various factors such as jurisdiction, relationship to the deceased, and tax laws. The rates used in these questions are fictional and provided for educational purposes.

1 Sarah inherited $500,000 from her late relative. If the inheritance tax rate is 10%, how much inheritance tax will Sarah owe?

2 Mark received an inheritance of $2,000,000 from his deceased parent. If the inheritance tax rate is 20%, how much inheritance tax will Mark owe?

3 Emily inherited a property with a fair market value of $1,500,000. If the inheritance tax rate is 15%, how much inheritance tax will Emily owe?

4 Michael received an inheritance of $800,000 in cash and investments. If the inheritance tax rate is 25%, how much inheritance tax will Michael owe?

5 David inherited a business worth $3,500,000 from his late relative. If the inheritance tax rate is 30%, how much inheritance tax will David owe?

6 Sarah inherited a property worth $750,000 and cash assets totaling $250,000 from her deceased relative. If the inheritance tax rate for properties is 10% and for cash assets is 5%, how much inheritance tax will Sarah owe?

7   Mark received an inheritance of $1,500,000 (50% in stocks and 50% in bonds). If the inheritance tax rate for stocks is 15% and for bonds is 20%, how much inheritance tax will Mark owe?

8   Emily inherited a family business worth $2,000,000 from her deceased parent. If the inheritance tax rate for family businesses is 5%, how much inheritance tax will Emily owe?

9   Michael received an inheritance of $800,000, which consists of a house valued at $600,000 and a bank account with $200,000. If the inheritance tax rate for houses is 10% and for bank accounts is 3%, how much inheritance tax will Michael owe?

10 David inherited an estate valued at $3,000,000, which includes real estate worth $2,000,000 and investment portfolios worth $1,000,000. If the inheritance tax rate for real estate is 20% and for investment portfolios is 15%, how much inheritance tax will David owe?

5.7 Corporate Tax

Corporate tax is usually based on the company's taxable income, which is calculated by deducting allowable expenses from the total revenue. The corporate tax rate varies from country to country and can have a significant impact on the company's financial standing and decision-making.

Please note that corporate tax rates can vary based on various factors such as jurisdiction, business type, and tax laws. The rates used in these questions are fictional and provided for educational purposes.

Let's try some corporate tax questions.

1   Marco Corporation has a taxable income of $500,000. If the corporate tax rate is 25%, how much corporate tax will Marco Corporation owe?

2   Gigi Corporation earned $1,200,000 in taxable income. If the corporate tax rate is 30%, how much corporate tax will Gigi Corporation owe?

3   Snacks Corporation has a taxable income of $750,000. If the corporate tax rate is 20%, how much corporate tax will Snacks Corporation owe?

4   Tweezie Corporation earned $2,500,000 in taxable income. If the corporate tax rate is 35%, how much corporate tax will Tweezie Corporation owe?

5   Sundip Corporation has a taxable income of $1,800,000. If the corporate tax rate is 28%, how much corporate tax will Sundip Corporation owe?

6   Lazy Corporation earned $400,000 in taxable income. If the corporate tax rate is 22%, how much corporate tax will Lazy Corporation owe?

7   Macky Corporation has a taxable income of $1,000,000. If the corporate tax rate is 32%, how much corporate tax will Macky Corporation owe?

8   Stylish Corporation earned $3,600,000 in taxable income. If the corporate tax rate is 29%, how much corporate tax will Stylish Corporation owe?

9   UVW Corporation has a taxable income of $550,000. If the corporate tax rate is 27%, how much corporate tax will UVW Corporation owe?

10 JKL Corporation earned $900,000 in taxable income. If the corporate tax rate is 24%, how much corporate tax will JKL Corporation owe?

11 ABC Corporation earned $500,000 in taxable income and has a tax deduction of $50,000. If the corporate tax rate is 25%, calculate the corporate tax liability.

12 Tracks Corporation has a taxable income of $800,000 and a tax credit of $100,000. If the corporate tax rate is 30%, determine the corporate tax liability.

13 MNO Corporation earned $1,200,000 in taxable income and has a tax deduction of $150,000. If the corporate tax rate is 20%, find the corporate tax liability.

14 Fawaz DXB earned AED 3,000,000 in taxable income and has a tax credit of AED 39,500. If the corporate tax rate is 12% what is the company's corporate tax liability?

UNIT 6

Managing Bank Accounts and Savings

Balancing and managing bank accounts is crucial in order to control your finances and make informed financial decisions:

- Accurate financial tracking allows you to identify any discrepancies, unauthorized transactions or errors, ensuring that your financial records are up-to-date and accurate.

- Effective account management helps you avoid costly fees and penalties. By keeping track of your account balance and monitoring transactions you can ensure you have sufficient funds to cover your expenses and avoid unnecessary fees that can be associated with a negative account balance or writing a check with insufficient funds.

- By reviewing your account statements and transaction history, you can analyze your spending patterns, identify areas for potential savings and allocate funds towards your financial goals.

- Regularly monitoring bank accounts helps you detect and prevent fraudulent activity. By promptly reviewing your transactions you can identify any unauthorized charges or suspicious activity and notify your bank or financial institution immediately to take appropriate action.

Let's try some questions.

1   Alex has a starting balance of $500 in his bank account. He withdraws $50 for groceries and deposits a paycheck of $200. Calculate his new balance.

2   Sarah has a bank account balance of $350. She spends $120 on shopping and deposits $200 from her part-time job. What is her new balance?

3   Mary's bank account has a current balance of $500. She receives a deposit of $300 and makes a withdrawal of $150. She also has a monthly direct debit of $50 for her phone bill. Will she have a positive or negative balance this month after these transactions?

4   John's bank account has a current balance of $800. He receives a deposit of $200 and makes a withdrawal of $300. He also has a monthly direct debit of $100 for his gym membership. Will he have a positive or negative balance this month after these transactions?

5   Sarah's bank account has a current balance of $350. She receives a deposit of $250 and makes a withdrawal of $400. She also has a monthly direct debit of $50 for her internet bill. Will she have a positive or negative balance this month after these transactions?

6   David's bank account has a current balance of $600. He receives a deposit of $400 and makes a withdrawal of $700. He also has a monthly direct debit of $100 for his credit card payment. Will he have a positive or negative balance after these transactions?

7   Emily's bank account has a current balance of $1,000. She receives a deposit of $500 and makes a withdrawal of $1,200. She also has a monthly direct debit of $150 for her utility bill. Will she have a positive or negative balance after these transactions?

8   Mark's bank account has a current balance of $700. He receives a deposit of $300 and makes a withdrawal of $800. He also has a monthly direct debit of $200 for his car loan payment. Will he have a positive or negative balance after these transactions?

9   Emma's bank account has a current balance of $1,200. She receives a deposit of $500 and makes a withdrawal of $1,500. She also has a monthly direct debit of $100 for her insurance premium. Will she have a positive or negative balance after these transactions?

10 Michael's bank account has a current balance of $900. He receives a deposit of $400 and makes a withdrawal of $1,000. He also has a monthly direct debit of $150 for his student loan payment. Will he have a positive or negative balance after these transactions?

11 Olivia's bank account has a current balance of $1,500. She receives a deposit of $600 and makes a withdrawal of $1,800. She also has a monthly direct debit of $200 for her car insurance payment. Will she have a positive or negative balance after these transactions?

12 Daniel's bank account has a current balance of $1,000. He receives a deposit of $500 and makes a withdrawal of $2,000. He also has a monthly direct debit of $150 for his subscription service. Will he have a positive or negative balance after these transactions?

13 Sireen wants to save money. She can either save $10 every week or $40 every month. After 6 months, which option would result in higher total savings?

14 Ali wants to save money. He can either save $2 a day or $14 a week. After one year, which option would result in higher total savings?

15 Majid wants to save money. He can either save $5 per day for one year or $200 every month for 6 months. Which option would result in higher total savings?

16 Joshua wants to save money. He can either save $1.50 every day or $10.00 every week. After 140 days, which option would result in higher total savings?

17 Emily wants to save money. She can either save $20 every week for 26 weeks or $80 every month for 6 months. Which option would result in higher total savings?

18 Adam wants to save money. He can either save $3 every day for 240 days or $21 every week for 8 months. Which option would result in higher total savings?

19 Abraham wants to save money. He can either save $2 per day, $14 per week, or $60 per month. If he plans to save for 5 years, which option would result in the highest total savings?

20 Jean-Paul wants to save money. He can either save $5 per day, $35 per week, or $150 per month. If he plans to save for 3 years, which option would result in the highest total savings?

21 Xianxi wants to save money. She can either save $3 per day, $21 per week, or $90 per month. If she plans to save for 8 years, which option would result in the highest total savings?

22 Aryan wants to save money. He can either save $1 per day, $7 per week, or $30 per month. If he plans to save for 2 years, which option would result in the highest total savings?

23 Sumitra wants to save money. She can either save $2 per day, $14 per week, or $60 per month. If she plans to save for 4 years, which option would result in the highest total savings?

24 Carlos wants to save money. He can either save $3 per day, $21 per week, or $90 per month. If he plans to save for 3 years, which option would result in the highest total savings?

25 Salma wants to save money. She can either save $2 per day, $10 per week, or $40 per month. If she plans to save for 3 years, which option would result in the highest total savings?

26 Zooloo wants to save money. He can either save $3 per day, $20 per week, or $80 per month. If he plans to save for 5 years, which option would result in the highest total savings?

27 Francois wants to save money. He can either save $1 per day, $7 per week, or $30 per month. If he plans to save for 4 years, which option would result in the highest total savings?

28 Diala wants to save money. She can either save $1.50 per day, $5 per week, or $40 per month. If she plans to save for 10 years, which option would result in the highest total savings?

29 Hisham wants to save money. He can either save $3 per day, $15 per week, or $80 per month. If he plans to save for 10 years, which option would result in the highest total savings?

30 Leyth wants to save money. He can either save $2 per day, $10 per week, or $50 per month. If he plans to save for 10 years, which option would result in the highest total savings?

31 Kamala wants to save money. She can either save $3 per day, $20 per week, or $100 per month. If she plans to save for 10 years, which option would result in the highest total savings?

32 Safa wants to save money. She can either save $2.50 per day, $15 per week, or $60 per month. If she plans to save for 10 years, which option would result in the highest total savings?

33 Michael wants to save money. He can either save $5 per day, $30 per week, or $200 per month. If he plans to save for 10 years, which option would result in the highest total savings?

Let's Explore

What should you look for when deciding what type of bank account to open? What bank account features would best suit your needs?

- Do you make frequent withdrawals or transfers? You will want to compare different bank account policies and fees associated with such transactions. For example, some banks allow unlimited ATM withdrawals if using their ATMs but will charge you for using other banks' ATMs.

- Are you concerned about not having sufficient funds in your account due to automatic debits or a post-dated check you may have forgotten that you wrote? Of course, the best way to avoid unnecessary NSF situations is to keep up-to-date with your expenses and budget accordingly. Sometimes it can be a timing issue. For example, you may get paid the third week of every month but have an automatic debit or check drawn from your account earlier in the month, which you may not have sufficient funds for at the time. In that case, you may want to inquire about overdraft protection options at your bank that link your checking account to another account (such as a savings account), credit card or line of credit, to cover the deficit in your checking account. However, each bank may have its own limits on how many times overdraft protection can be used.

● What is your bank's policy on providing fraud protection to its customers? You should become familiar with your bank's policies and procedures in case you notice suspicious activity with your account. Although banks normally offer protection if a customer is the victim of fraudulent activity, they may impose a specific timeframe for customers to report unauthorized transactions in order to qualify for full protection.

● What are the fees and processing time at your bank associated with different transactions? In some cases, you may be able to transact using a post-dated check. However, there may be instances where the payee requires a manager's check or bank draft, which your bank would typically charge you for.

● Are you considering applying for a credit card, loan or mortgage? You will definitely want to compare interest rates and features offered by different financial institutions. For example, some credit cards offer discounts or rewards when used at specific establishments.

UNIT 7

Interest

Interest refers to the additional amount of money charged or earned on a loan, investment, or deposit. It is a percentage of the principal amount, which is the initial sum of money paid. When you borrow money, interest is the cost you pay for using the funds, typically expressed as an annual percentage. On the other hand, when you invest or deposit money, interest is the return or earnings you receive on top of your initial investment. Understanding interest is important as it affects the cost of borrowing and the potential growth of savings or investments.

7.1 Simple Interest

Simple interest is a straightforward method of calculating interest on a principal amount over a set period of time. It is calculated based on the initial sum (the principal), interest rate (usually expressed as a percentage) and the duration for which the interest is calculated (usually in years).

Try the following questions using the following formula:

Simple Interest = Principal x Rate x Time

1. Find the simple interest on a loan of $2,500 at an interest rate of 8% per year for 3 years.

2. If you deposit $1,000 in a savings account that earns 5% interest per year, how much interest will you earn after 2 years?

3. Bob borrowed $3,000 from a friend and agreed to pay an interest rate of 10% per year for 1 ½ years. How much interest will Bob pay?

4. You invested $5,000 in a bond that pays 6% interest per year for 4 years. How much interest will you earn?

5   Sarah borrowed $800 from her parents and agreed to pay an interest rate of 7.5% per year for 2 years. How much interest will Sarah pay?

6   If you deposit $2,500 in a savings account that earns 4% interest per year, how much interest will you earn after 3 years?

7   John borrowed $1,200 from a bank and agreed to pay an interest rate of 9% per year for 2 ½ years. How much interest will John pay?

8   You invested $4,000 in a mutual fund that pays 5.5% interest per year for 5 years. How much interest will you earn?

9   Mary borrowed $2,500 from a friend and agreed to pay an interest rate of 6% per year for 1 ½ years. How much interest will Mary pay?

10 If you deposit $3,000 in a savings account that earns 3.5% interest per year, how much interest will you earn after 4 years?

11 Bob borrowed $4,500 from a bank and agreed to pay an interest rate of 7.25% per year for 3 years. How much interest will Bob pay?

12 You invested $6,000 in a certificate of deposit that pays 4.75% interest per year for 2 ½ years. How much interest will you earn?

13 Sarah borrowed $1,000 from her parents and agreed to pay an interest rate of 6.5% per year for 1 year. How much interest will Sarah pay?

14 If you deposit $5,000 in a savings account that earns 2.25% interest per year, how much interest will you earn after 3 ½ years?

15 John borrowed $1,500 from a bank and agreed to pay an interest rate of 8.75% per year for 2 years. How much interest will John pay?

16 You invested $2,000 in a bond that pays 3.25% interest per year for 4 ½ years. How much interest will you earn?

17 Mary borrowed $2,200 from a friend and agreed to pay an interest rate of 5.5% per year for 3 years. How much interest will Mary pay?

18 If you deposit $4,500 in a savings account that earns 4% interest per year, how much interest will you earn after 2 ½ years?

19 Bob borrowed $3,800 from a bank and agreed to pay an interest rate of 6.25% per year for 1 ½ years. How much interest will Bob pay?

20 You invested $5,500 in a mutual fund that pays 4.5% interest per year for 5 years. How much interest will you earn?

21 Sarah deposits $500 in a savings account that earns annual simple interest at a rate of 5%. How much savings will she have after 3 years?

22 Anna deposits $200 in a savings account that earns annual simple interest at a rate of 4%. How much savings will she have after 2 years?

23 John deposits $1,500 in a savings account that earns annual simple interest at a rate of 2.5%. How much savings will he have after 4 years?

7.2 Compound Interest

Compound interest is a more complex method of calculating interest because it not only takes into account the initial principal and interest rate, but also the interest that accumulates over time.

Use the following formula for calculating compound interest:

$$A = P\left(1 + \frac{r}{n}\right)^{(nt)}$$

$$Interest = A - P$$

Let's define each term in the formula:

A: The future value or total amount, including both the principal amount and the accumulated interest over time.

P: The principal amount, which refers to the initial investment or the initial loan amount.

r: The annual interest rate, represented as a decimal. It is the percentage charged or earned on the principal amount over one year.

n: The number of compounding periods per year. Compounding refers to how frequently the interest is added to the principal. Common values for n include 1 (annual compounding), 2 (semi-annual), 4 (quarterly), or 12 (monthly).

t: The number of years or the time period over which the interest is calculated.

By using this formula, you can determine the future value or total amount after a specific period, taking into account compound interest.

The first question has been solved for you.

1 Calculate the compound interest on $5,000 invested at an annual interest rate of 5% for 3 years, compounded annually.

SOLUTION

Compound Interest $= P\left(1 + \frac{r}{n}\right)^{(1*3)} - P$

Compound Interest $= \$5,000 \left(1 + \frac{0.05}{1}\right)^{(1*3)} - P$

Compound Interest $= \$5,000(1.05)^3 - \$5,000$

Compound Interest $= \$5,000(1.157625) - \$5,000$

Compound Interest $= \$5,788.13 - \$5,000$

Compound Interest $= \$788.13$

2   If you invest $2,000 at an annual interest rate of 4.5% for 5 years, compounded annually, how much interest will you earn?

3   Calculate the compound interest on $10,000 invested at an annual interest rate of 6% for 2 years, compounded quarterly.

4   If you invest $3,500 at an annual interest rate of 3.75% for 4 years, compounded quarterly, how much interest will you earn?

5   Calculate the compound interest on $7,000 invested at an annual interest rate of 4.25% for 3 years, compounded semi-annually.

6   If you invest $4,200 at an annual interest rate of 5.5% for 6 years, compounded monthly, how much interest will you earn?

7   Calculate the compound interest on $12,000 invested at an annual interest rate of 7% for 5 years, compounded annually.

8   If you invest $6,500 at an annual interest rate of 4.75% for 4 years, compounded quarterly, how much interest will you earn?

9   Calculate the compound interest on $9,500 invested at an annual interest rate of 6.5% for 3 years, compounded monthly.

10 If you invest $8,000 at an annual interest rate of 3.25% for 5 years, compounded semi-annually, how much interest will you earn?

11 Calculate the future investment value (principal plus interest earned) if $11,000 is invested at an annual compound interest rate of 4% for 2 years, compounded annually.

12 If you invest $10,500 at an annual interest rate of 5.75% for 4 years, compounded semi-annually, what will the future value of your investment (principal + interest) be?

13 Calculate the future value of the investment (principal + interest) if $13,500 is invested at an annual interest rate of 6.25% for 3 years, compounded annually.

14 If you invest $15,000 at an annual interest rate of 4.5% for 5 years, compounded annually, what will the future value of your investment (principal + interest) be?

15 Calculate the compound interest on $17,500 invested at an annual interest rate of 5.5% for 3 years, compounded annually.

16 If you invest $20,000 at an annual interest rate of 3.75% for 4 years, compounded semi-annually, how much interest will you earn?

17 Calculate the compound interest on $22,500 invested at an annual interest rate of 4.75% for 3 years, compounded monthly.

18 If you invest $25,000 at an annual interest rate of 4.25% for 5 years, compounded annually, what will the future value of your investment be?

19 Calculate the compound interest on $27,500 invested at an annual interest rate of 5.25% for 4 years, compounded annually.

20 If you invest $30,000 at an annual interest rate of 5.5% for 3 years, compounded monthly, how much interest will you earn?

7.3 Interest on Savings (Simple and Compound)

1 Sarah deposits $500 in a savings account that earns annual simple interest at a rate of 5%. What is her total savings after 3 years?

2 Mark deposits $1,000 in a savings account that earns a monthly compound annual interest at a rate of 3%. What is the future value of her savings after 5 years?

3 Anna deposits $200 in a savings account that earns a simple annual interest rate of 4%. How much will her savings grow to after 2 years?

4 John deposits $1,500 in a savings account that earns a simple annual interest rate of 2.5%. What will his balance be after 4 years?

5 Emma deposits $300 in a savings account that earns an annual simple interest rate of 6%. What will her total savings be after 1 year?

6 David deposits $2,000 in a savings account that earns an annual interest rate of 4.5%, compounded semi-annually. How much money will he have in his account after 3 years?

7 Lisa deposits $400 in a savings account that earns a simple annual interest rate of 2%. How much savings will she have after 5 years?

8 Mike deposits AED 3,500 in a savings account that earns an annual interest rate of 3.5%, compounded monthly. How much savings will he have after 2 years?

9 Rachel deposits $600 in a savings account that earns an annual simple interest rate of 1.5%. What will her total savings be after 4 years?

10 Tom deposits GBP 4,000 in a savings account that earns an annual interest rate of 2%, compounded quarterly. How much savings will he accumulate after 3 years?

11 Lily deposits 500 EUD in a savings account that earns an annual simple interest rate of 4%. What will her total savings be after 5 years?

12 Alex deposits JOD 1,200 in a savings account that earns an annual interest rate of 3.5%, compounded quarterly. How much will he have in his account after 2 years?

UNIT 8

Investing

8.1 Return on Investments

Return on investment (ROI) is a financial metric used to measure the profitability and efficiency of an investment. It provides a way to evaluate the financial performance of an investment by comparing the return (gain or profit) generated from the investment to the initial cost or investment amount.

ROI is typically expressed as a percentage or ratio and represents the net gain or loss from an investment relative to the initial investment amount. The formula for calculating ROI is as follows:

$$ROI = \left(\frac{Net\ Gain\ from\ Investment}{Initial\ Investment\ Cost} \right) \times 100$$

The net gain from the investment is calculated by subtracting the initial investment cost from the final value of the investment, which includes any income, dividends, or capital appreciation.

For example, if you invest $10,000 in a stock and sell it after a year for $12,000, your net gain would be $2,000. Using the ROI formula, the calculation would be:

$$ROI = (\$2{,}000/\$10{,}000) \times 100 = 20\%$$

This means that your ROI for the investment is 20%. In other words, for every dollar invested, you earned a 20% return.

ROI is a useful metric for evaluating the profitability of investments and comparing different investment opportunities. A higher ROI indicates a more favorable investment, as it represents a greater return relative to the initial investment cost. However, it's important to consider the time frame, risk, and other factors associated with the investment to make a comprehensive assessment of its performance.

ROI can be applied to various types of investments, including stocks, bonds, real estate, business ventures, and more. It helps investors and businesses make informed decisions regarding the allocation of resources and the potential profitability of their investments.

Let's try some questions now.

1   An investment of $5,000 grows to $7,500 after 3 years. Calculate the rate of return on this investment.

2   John invested $2,000, and after 2 years, his investment grew to $2,500. What is the rate of return on his investment?

3   An investment of $10,000 increased to $12,500 after 5 years. Determine the rate of return on this investment.

4   Samantha invested $1,500, and her investment grew to $2,000 after 4 years. What is the rate of return on her investment?

5   An investment of $20,000 yields a final value of $24,000 after 2 years. Determine the rate of return on this investment.

6   Jane invested $3,000, and after 3 years, her investment grew to $3,600. Calculate the rate of return on her investment.

7   An investment of $15,000 increased to $19,500 after 4 years. Determine the rate of return on this investment.

8   Mike invested $4,000, and his investment grew to $4,800 after 5 years. What is the rate of return on his investment?

9   An investment of $25,000 yields a final value of $32,500 after 3 years. Calculate the rate of return on this investment.

10   Mark invested $10,000, and after 4 years, his investment grew to $12,000. Determine the rate of return on his investment.

11   An investment of $7,500 increased to $9,000 after 2 years. What is the rate of return on this investment?

12   Rachel invested $6,000, and her investment grew to $7,500 after 3 years. Calculate the rate of return on her investment.

13   An investment of $12,000 yields a final value of $15,000 after 4 years. Determine the rate of return on this investment.

14 Ibrahim invested $8,000, and after 2 years, his investment grew to $9,600. What is the rate of return on his investment?

15 An investment of $20,000 increased to $24,000 after 3 years. Calculate the rate of return on this investment

16 Sarah invested $3,500, and her investment grew to $4,200 after 2 years. Determine the rate of return on her investment.

17 An investment of $15,000 yields a final value of $18,750 after 5 years. What is the rate of return on this investment?

18 David invested $5,000, and after 3 years, his investment grew to $6,500. Calculate the rate of return on his investment.

19 An investment of $10,000 increased to $13,000 after 4 years. Determine the rate of return on this investment.

20 Emily invested $2,500, and her investment grew to $3,000 after 2 years. What is the rate of return on her investment?

21 You invested $5,000 in a stock, and after one year, the value dropped to $4,500. What is the rate of return?

22 You purchased a bond for $10,000, and after two years, its value decreased to $8,500. What is the rate of return?

23 You invested $2,000 in a mutual fund, and after three years, your investment value dropped to $1,500. What is the rate of return?

24 You purchased a cryptocurrency for $1,000, and after six months, its value declined to $600. What is the rate of return?

25 You acquired 100 shares of a company's stock for $50 per share, and after four years, the stock price dropped to $30 per share. What is the rate of return?

26 You invested $10,000 in residential property, and over five years, its value declined to $8,000. What is the rate of return?

27 You purchased a collectible item for $1,500, and after three years, its value dropped to $1,200. What is the rate of return?

28 You invested $1,000 in a savings account, and after two years, the balance dropped to $800. What is the rate of return?

29 You purchased a vintage car for $20,000, and after four years, its value declined to $16,000. What is the rate of return?

30 You acquired 500 shares of a company's stock for $5 per share, and after three years, the stock price dropped to $3 per share. What is the rate of return?

8.2 Compounding Investments

Compounding investments refer to a strategy where the returns or earnings generated from an investment are reinvested to generate additional returns over time. In simple terms, it means earning returns not only on the initial investment but also on the accumulated earnings from previous periods. (We calculated compounding investments earlier when we learned about compound interest).

The power of compounding lies in the fact that as the investment grows, the potential for earning returns also increases. The returns earned in one period become part of the principal amount for the next period, allowing for exponential growth over an extended period.

Here's an example to illustrate the concept of compounding investments:

Let's say you invest $10,000 in a compounding investment with an annual interest rate of 5%. At the end of the first year, you would earn $500 in interest (5% of $10,000). Instead of withdrawing the interest, you reinvest it back into the investment, resulting in a new principal amount of $10,500 for the second year. In the second year, you would earn 5% interest on this new amount, which is $525. The process continues, with the interest earned each year being added to the principal and earning additional returns.

Over time, compounding can have a significant impact on the growth of investments, especially when compounded over long periods. As the investment grows and compounds, the rate of growth can accelerate, leading to exponential growth and larger returns in later years.

It's important to note that compounding can occur with various types of investments, such as stocks, bonds, mutual funds or savings accounts. The specific compounding frequency (e.g. annually, quarterly, monthly) and the interest rate or investment returns will determine the rate at which the investment grows.

Let's try some questions. The first one has been solved for you.

1. John invests $5,000 in a savings account that earns an annual interest rate of 4.5%. How much will his investment be worth after 5 years, assuming the interest is compounded annually?

   SOLUTION

   Future value $(FV) = P \times \left(1 + \frac{r}{n}\right)^{(nt)}$

   Principal amount (P) = $5,000

   Annual interest rate (r) = 4.5% = 0.045

   Number of compounding periods per year (n) = 1

   Number of years (t) = 5

   Future value $(FV) = P \times \left(1 + \frac{r}{n}\right)^{(nt)}$

   FV = $5,000 $\times$ (1 + 0.045/1)$^{(1*5)}$

   FV = $5,000 $\times$ (1.246181938)

   FV $\approx$ $6,230.91

   After 5 years, John's investment will be worth approximately $6,230.91.

2. Emma invests $10,000 in a mutual fund that has an annual growth rate of 7%. If the growth is compounded quarterly, what will be the value of her investment after 3 years?

3   Sarah invests $2,500 in a bond that offers a fixed annual interest rate of 6.25%. If the interest is compounded semi-annually, what will be the value of her investment after 2 years?

4   Michael invests $1,000 in a stock that has an annual return of 9%. If the returns are compounded monthly, what will be the value of his investment after 5 years?

5   Linda invests $7,500 in a certificate of deposit that offers an annual interest rate of 3.75%. If the interest is compounded annually, what will be the value of her investment after 4 years?

6   Assume that you invest $1, 000,000 at 20% interest per year. Calculate the future value of your investment after one year based on a varying number of compounding periods.

   A   Annual compounding interest

   B   Semi-annual compounding interest

   C   Quarterly compounding interest

   D   Monthly compounding interest

7   Maryam and Josh each have $5,000 to invest separately. Maryam decides to invest her money with a financial institution that will offer her 7% annual interest rate, compounded monthly. Josh decides to invest his money at 7% annual interest rate, compounded annually. Calculate the future value of each investment after two years.

8   Assume you invest $1,000 at a 6% annual interest rate, compounded annually. If you reinvest all your money at the same interest rate, how much would you have in total by the end of the (a) first year and (b) second year?

9   The "rule of 72" is a quick way to learn how long it will take to double your money. The rule of 72 factors in the length of time and interest rate you have your money invested at. To apply this rule, you multiply the number of years you plan to invest your money for by the interest rate. When the product is 72, your money is doubled. However, please note that the rule of 72 only provides a rough estimate and may not be accurate for different compounding frequencies.

Let's try the rule of 72 in the following scenarios:

A   You have $2,000 saved at a 4% annual interest rate. (i) How long will it take to double your money? (ii) What if the interest rate was 10%?

B   You have $700 and want to double your money in 10 years. At what annual interest rate would your money double in (i) 5 years, (ii)10 years or (iii) 15 years?

8.3 Cryptocurrency

Cryptocurrency is a digital or virtual form of currency that does not use banks to verify transactions. It uses cryptography to secure financial transactions and operates on decentralized networks called blockchain, which ensure transparency, security, and immutability.

Let's try some questions related to cryptocurrency.

1   Bob bought 5 Bitcoins at a price of $10,000 per Bitcoin. The transaction fee for buying and selling Bitcoins is 2% of the total transaction value. If Bob sells all his Bitcoins when the price reaches $15,000 per Bitcoin, what is his total profit or loss after considering the transaction fees?

2   Alice invested $5,000 in a cryptocurrency that offers an annual interest rate of 8%. How much money will Alice have after 2 years if the interest is compounded annually?

3   A cryptocurrency has a total supply of 10 million coins. In the first year, the mining rewards are set at 1,000 coins per day. What is the percentage of the mining rewards compared to the total supply in the first year?

4   Sarah purchased 500 units of a cryptocurrency at a price of $0.50 per unit. If the price of the cryptocurrency increases to $1.20 per unit, what is the percentage increase in Sarah's investment?

5   Jackson purchased 100 units of a cryptocurrency at a price of $0.20 per unit. The price later increased to $0.40 per unit, but Jackson decided to sell only 50% of his holdings. What is the amount Jackson profited from selling the cryptocurrency?

6   Emma bought 200 units of a cryptocurrency at a price of $1.00 per unit. The price later decreased to $0.80 per unit, and she decided to sell all her holdings. What is the percentage loss on her investment?

7   Alex invested $5,000 in a cryptocurrency and earned a return of 15% over one year. What is the final investment value after one year?

8   Lily purchased 50 units of a cryptocurrency at a price of $2.50 per unit. The price later increased to $3.75 per unit, and she decided to sell 43 units. What is the total amount Lily received from selling the cryptocurrency?

9   Ethan invested $3,000 in a cryptocurrency and experienced a growth rate of 10% per month, compounded monthly. After 6 months, what is the total investment value?

10 Ethan makes another investment of $3,000 in cryptocurrency. However, this one experiences a growth rate of 10% annually, compounded monthly. After 6 months, what is the total investment value?

UNIT 9

Debt Management

Debt management involves effectively handling various types of debt, such as credit card debt, college loans, personal loans and car loans. Managing debt effectively is crucial to avoid penalties and minimize interest payments.

Here are a few points to consider:

- Make sure to pay your debt obligations on time to avoid late payment penalties and additional fees. Set up automatic payments or create reminders to ensure you do not miss a due date.

- Focus on paying off high-interest debt first, such as credit card balances, as they tend to accrue more interest over time. By tackling these debts aggressively, you can save money on interest payments in the long run.

- Create a realistic budget that includes debt repayments. Allocate a portion of your income towards paying down debts systematically. By incorporating debt payments into your budget, you can manage your cash flow effectively and ensure you have enough funds to cover your obligations.

- Paying only the minimum amount due on your debts can result in a long repayment period and higher interest payments. Whenever possible, pay more than the minimum payment to accelerate debt repayment and minimize interest charges.

9.1 Credit Cards

Let's take a closer look at managing credit card debt through these math problems.

1   Samantha's credit card has a balance of $10,000. Her credit card company charges an annual interest rate of 17%. Calculate (a) the daily interest rate and (b) the balance on day two of her billing cycle.

2   Brian has an average daily balance of $1,200 on his credit card. The credit card company charges an annual interest rate of 16%. If there are 30 days in the billing cycle, how much will he be charged in interest during the current billing cycle?

3   Emily has a credit card balance of $3,500. If she makes monthly payments of $200, how many months will it take for Emily to pay off her debt?

4   Your credit card company requires you to pay 3% of your outstanding loan balance. You owe $6,000 on your credit card. Calculate your minimum payment.

5   Daniel has a credit card balance of $4,000. If he wants to pay off his debt in 36 months, what should his monthly payment be?

6   Sophia owes $2,800 on her credit card. If she wants to pay off her debt in 12 months, what should her monthly payment be?

7   You made a purchase of $200 on your credit card with an interest rate of 18% per year. If you pay off the entire balance in one month, how much interest will you pay?

8   You have a credit card with a balance of $500 and an interest rate of 20% per year. If you make a payment of $100, how much interest will you owe after one month?

9   Michelle's opening credit card balance is $1600 and she purchases $631 and repays $419. If the credit card company requires a minimum payment of 8% of the closing balance, find the minimum payment required.

10 Ibrahim has a credit card with a 19.5% annual interest rate and a 2% minimum monthly payment requirement. Ibrahim accumulates a balance of $3,150. What would be the minimum monthly payment at the end of the first month?

11 Sara has a credit card with an interest rate of 18% per year. If she has an outstanding balance of $500, how much interest will she be charged after 1 month?

12 Maya's credit card had a balance of $305.62 in June. She subsequently made a payment of $125 and purchased a bag for $290. Her credit card company charges an annual interest rate of 43.2%. Calculate the interest charge at the end of the month.

13 Jessica has a credit card with an annual interest rate of 18%. If her outstanding balance is $800, what will the interest charge be after two months if no prior payments are made?

14 Daniel has a credit card with an annual interest rate of 20%. If he has an outstanding balance of $2,500, (a) how much interest will he be charged after 2 months if he does not make any prior payments, and (b) what is the total amount he must pay if a 1% penalty fee is charged on the total balance after the second month?

15 Emily has a credit card with an outstanding balance of $2,500. The credit card company requires a minimum monthly payment of 3% of the outstanding balance or $50, whichever is higher. Calculate the minimum payment for this month.

16 Jason has a credit card with an interest rate of 24% per year. If he has an outstanding balance of $3,000, how much interest will he be charged after 3 months if no prior payments are made?

17 Sarah has a credit card with an annual interest rate of 16%. If her outstanding balance is $1,500, what will the interest charge be after 45 days if no prior payments are made?

18 Michael has a credit card with an opening balance of $2,650 and purchases $277 and repays $30. If the minimum payment required is 21% of the closing balance, find the minimum payment required.

19 Emma has a credit card balance of $3,560 and repays $300, what is her minimum monthly payment if the credit card company requires a 2% payment?

20 If Federer's credit card company charges an annual 6.5% interest rate, what is the daily interest rate?

21 Alexis purchases a handbag for $2,500 and a pair of boots for $600 on her credit card, which charges 18% annual interest rate. What is the total interest owed after 40 days if no prior payments are made?

22 Grace has a credit card with an annual interest rate of 14%. If her outstanding balance is $2,000, what is the daily interest on this balance?

23 Matthew has a credit card with an interest rate of 21% per year. If he has an outstanding balance of $3,000, how much will he owe including balance and interest after one month?

24 Sophia has a credit card with an annual interest rate of 18%. If her outstanding balance is $1,200, how much will she owe after 50 days?

25 Elon has a credit card with an annual interest rate of 42%. His credit card balance was 0 until the end of June when he purchased an item for $622. His monthly minimum payment is 9% of the balance.

A Calculate his minimum payment for June.

B Calculate the interest on the remaining balance.

C Calculate the end of July balance (including interest incurred) after paying the June minimum payment.

D Calculate the minimum payment for July.

26 Suppose that your credit card calculates interest using an annual interest rate of 44%. Your previous credit card statement had a balance of $340. So, you make a payment of $110. The next day, you use your credit card to purchase a new laptop for $1,215. Use this information to fill out the table below (including calculating the interest amount and new balance):

	Previous Balance	Payments	Purchases	Interest	New Balance
Month 1					

27 Continuing the same scenario from the previous question, assume that you make another payment of $85 and then use your credit card to purchase a mobile phone for $450. Us this information to complete the following table (including calculating the interest amount and new balance):

	Previous Balance	Payments	Purchases	Interest	New Balance
Month 1					

9.2 Loans

When borrowing or lending money, it is crucial to ensure clarity regarding whether the transaction is a loan or a gift. Here is a summary of important points to consider:

- Intent and Communication: Clearly communicate your intentions and expectations with the other party involved. Discuss whether the money is intended as a loan that must be repaid or as a gift with no expectation of repayment. Open and honest communication is essential to avoid misunderstandings and potential conflicts.

- Written Agreement: Regardless of whether it is a loan or a gift, consider documenting the transaction with a written agreement. A loan agreement should outline the loan amount, repayment terms (including interest, if applicable), and any other relevant conditions. For a gift, a written acknowledgment or gift letter can help clarify that the funds are not expected to be repaid.

- Terms and Conditions: For a loan, clearly define the terms and conditions, including the repayment schedule, interest rate (if any), late payment penalties, and any other relevant provisions. Both parties should have a clear understanding of their responsibilities and obligations.

- Legal Considerations: It is advisable to consult legal professionals to ensure compliance with applicable laws and regulations.

They can provide guidance on drafting loan agreements, gift documentation, and any legal implications or tax considerations associated with the transaction.

- Repayment Plan: If it is a loan, establish a repayment plan that suits both parties' financial circumstances. Determine the frequency and amount of payments, and document these details in the loan agreement. Regular communication regarding repayment progress can help maintain a positive relationship.

- Gift Tax Implications: If it is a gift, be aware of any potential gift tax implications. In some jurisdictions, gifts above a certain threshold may be subject to gift taxes. Consult tax professionals or relevant authorities to understand the applicable regulations in your specific situation.

- Financial Impact: Both borrowers and lenders should consider the potential financial impact of the transaction. Borrowers must evaluate their ability to meet repayment obligations, while lenders should assess the impact on their own financial situation and liquidity.

By ensuring clarity regarding whether a transaction is a loan or a gift and taking appropriate steps to document the agreement, establish repayment terms (if applicable), and address legal considerations, both parties can protect their interests and maintain a clear understanding of their financial obligations.

a. Simple Interest Loans

There are different formulas for calculating loan payments, depending on the type of loan and terms of repayment. Simple interest loans are commonly used for shorter-term loans or loans where interest is calculated based on a simplified method. Personal loans used for personal expenses or small business loans with shorter term, may be structured as simple interest loans.

To calculate the monthly payment on a simple interest loan, you can follow these steps:

Step 1: Calculate the interest accrued over the loan term
Interest = Principal x Rate x Time

Step 2: Calculate the total amount to be repaid
Total Amount = Principal + Interest

Step 3: Calculate the monthly payment
Monthly Payment = Total Amount/(time x 12)

Let's try an example:

1   You borrow $5,000 at an annual interest rate of 4.5% for a period of 2 years. Calculate (a) the total amount to be repaid and (b) the monthly payment.

SOLUTION

Step 1: Calculate the total interest accrued.

Principal x Rate x Time Interest = $5,000 x 0.045 x 2 = $450

Step 2: Calculate the total amount to be repaid.

Total Amount = *Principal + Interest*

Total Amount = $5,000 + $450 = $5,450

Step 3: Calculate the monthly payment.

Total Amount/(Time x 12)

Monthly Payment = $5,450/(2 x 12) = $227.08

Therefore, (a) the total amount to be repaid is $5,450, and (b) the monthly payment is $227.08.

Now, try the following problems.

2   You take out a loan of $10,000 with a 6% annual interest rate for 3.5 years (42 months). Find (a) the total interest paid and (b) the fixed monthly payment.

3   Principal: $8,500 Annual Interest Rate (Rate): 3.75% Time: 4 years. Find (a) the total amount to be repaid and (b) the fixed monthly payment.

4   Principal: $15,000 Rate: 5.25% Time: 2 1/2 years. Find (a) the total amount to be repaid and (b) the fixed monthly payment.

5   Principal: $12,500 Rate: 4% Time: 6 years. Find (a) the total amount to be repaid and (b) the monthly payment.

6   Principal: $20,000 Rate: 6.5% Time: 1 1/2 years (18 months). Find (a) the total amount to be repaid and (b) the monthly payment.

7   Principal: $6,000 Rate: 2.25% Time: 3 years. Calculate (a) the total amount to be repaid and (b) the monthly payment.

8   Principal: $9,500 Rate: 4.75% Time: 2 years. Calculate (a) the total amount to be repaid and (b) the monthly payment.

9   Principal: $25,000 Rate: 7% Time: 5 years. Calculate (a) the total amount to be repaid and (b) the monthly payment.

10 Principal: $7,500 Rate: 3.5% Time: 4 1/2 years. Calculate (a) the total amount to be repaid and (b) the monthly payment.

11 Principal: $18,000 Rate: 5% Time: 3 years. Find (a) the total amount to be repaid and (b) the monthly payment.

12 Principal: $10,500 Rate: 4.25% Time: 2.75 years (33 months). Find (a) the total amount to be repaid and (b) the monthly payment.

13 Principal: $14,000 Rate: 3.9% Time: 4.25 years (51 months). Find (a) the total amount to be repaid and (b) the monthly payment.

14 Principal: $8,000 Rate: 4.5% Time: 3.5 years (42 months). Find (a) the total amount to be repaid and (b) the monthly payment.

15 Principal: $11,200 Rate: 5.75% Time: 2.25 years (27 months). Find (a) the total amount to be repaid and (b) the monthly payment.

b. Compound Interest Loans

Use the following formula for calculating compound interest loans:

$$A = P(1 + r/n)^{(nt)}$$
$$\text{Interest} = A - P$$

1. You take out a loan of $10,000 with a 6% annual interest rate, compounded monthly, for 3.5 years (42 months). Find (a) the total interest to be paid and (b) the fixed monthly payment.

2. Principal: $8,500 Rate: 3.75%, compounded monthly Time: 4 years. Find (a) the total interest to be paid and (b) the fixed monthly payment.

3. Principal: $15,000 Rate: 5.25%, compounded monthly Time: 2 1/2 years. Find (a) the total interest to be paid and (b) the fixed monthly payment.

4. Principal: $12,500 Rate: 4%, compounded monthly Time: 6 years. Find (a) the total interest to be paid and (b) the monthly payment.

5. Principal: $20,000 Rate: 6.5%, compounded monthly Time: 1.5 years (18 months). Find (a) the total interest to be paid and (b) the monthly payment.

6. Principal: $6,000 Rate: 2.25%, compounded monthly Time: 3 years. Calculate (a) the total interest to be paid and (b) the monthly payment.

7. Principal: $9,500 Rate: 4.75%, compounded monthly Time: 2 years. Calculate (a) the total interest to be paid and (b) the monthly payment.

8. Principal: $25,000 Rate: 7%, compounded monthly Time: 5 years. Calculate (a) the total interest to be paid and (b) the monthly payment.

9. Principal: $7,500 Rate: 3.5%, compounded monthly Time: 4.5 years (54 months). Calculate (a) the total interest to be paid and (b) the monthly payment.

10 Principal: $18,000 Rate: 5%, compounded monthly Time: 3 years. Find (a) the total interest to be paid and (b) the monthly payment.

11 Principal: $10,500 Rate: 4.25%, compounded monthly Time: 2.75 years (33 months). Find (a) the total amount to be repaid and (b) the monthly payment.

Let's Explore

12 Let's compare two loan options: a simple interest loan and a compound interest loan. Consider a $10,000 loan at 5% interest repaid over five years.

  A Calculate the cost of borrowing (principal + interest) if it is a simple interest loan.

  B Calculate the cost of borrowing (principal + interest) if interest is compounded monthly.

  C Compare the results of (a) and (b) and think about other factors to consider when making a decision to take out a loan.

c. Amortized Loan Formula

The following amortization formula is used for loans with equal monthly payments that include both principal and interest. The formula calculates the payment amount based on the loan amount, interest rate and loan term.

$$M = P \times (r \times (1 + r)^n) / ((1 + r)^n - 1)$$

Let's break down the formula used to calculate the monthly payment on a loan:

M: Monthly payment

P: Loan principal (amount borrowed)

r: Monthly interest rate

n: Total number of payments

The formula is derived from the concept of an amortizing loan, where each monthly payment consists of both principal (the amount borrowed) and interest (the cost of borrowing). The goal is to distribute the repayment of the loan over a fixed number of monthly payments.

Here's how the formula works step by step:

- Step 1: Convert the annual interest rate to a monthly interest rate. To calculate the monthly interest rate (r), you divide the annual interest rate by 12 and convert it to a decimal. For example, if the annual interest rate is 6%, the monthly interest rate would be 0.06/12 = 0.005.

- Step 2: Determine the total number of payments. Multiply the number of years (n) by 12 to get the total number of payments. For example, for a 30-year loan, the total number of payments would be 30 x 12 = 360.

- Step 3: Calculate the numerator. Multiply the loan principal (P) by the monthly interest rate (r) and then multiply it by (1 + r) raised to the power of the total number of payments (n).

- Step 4: Calculate the denominator. Calculate (1 + r) raised to the power of the total number of payments (n) and subtract 1.

- Step 5: Divide the numerator by the denominator and multiply the result by P, to get the monthly payment (M).

It's important to note that this monthly payment calculation assumes fixed interest rates and equal monthly payments throughout the loan term. Additional fees or changes in interest rates may affect the actual loan payments.

1 Megan wants to finance a car and is considering a loan of $25,000. The bank offers her an interest rate of 4.5% per year for a term of 5 years. Calculate Megan's monthly car loan payment.

SOLUTION

Step 1: Convert the annual interest rate to a monthly interest rate.

Annual interest rate = 4.5% = 0.045 (*as a decimal*)

Monthly interest rate = 0.045/12 = 0.00375

Step 2: Convert the loan term to months.

Loan term (n) = 5 *years* × 12 *months/year* = 60 *months*

Step 3: Use the amortization formula to calculate the monthly payment.

Principal loan amount (P) = $25,000

Monthly Payment = $P \times (r(1+r)^n) / ((1+r)^n - 1)$

Plugging in the values:

$25{,}000 \times (0.00375(1+0.00375)^{60}) / ((1+0.00375)^{60} - 1)$

Step 4: Simplify the equation.

Calculate $(1+0.00375)^{60}$ and $((1+0.00375)^{60} - 1)$ separately.

$(1+0.00375)^{60} = 1.251795821$

$(1+0.00375)^{60} - 1 = 0.251795821$

Monthly Payment = $25{,}000 \times (0.00375 \times 1.251795821)/0.251795821$

Step 5: Calculate the monthly payment.

Monthly Payment = $466.08 (*rounded to two decimal places*)

Therefore, Megan's monthly car loan payment for a $25,000 loan at an interest rate of 4.5% for 5 years is $466.08.

2 Michael wants to purchase a car and decides to take a loan of $20,000. The bank offers him a loan with an annual interest rate of 6.25% for a term of 4 years. Calculate Michael's monthly car loan payment.

3 You decide to get a car with a loan. *Car loan Amount:* $15,000 *Annual Interest Rate (Rate):* 5% *Loan Term:* 3 years. What is your monthly payment?

4 Calculate the monthly payment: *Car loan Amount:* $22,500 *Rate:* 6.75% *Loan Term:* 5 years.

5 Calculate the monthly payment: *Car loan Amount:* $12,000 *Rate:* 4.25% *Loan Term:* 2 years.

6 *Car loan amount:* $18,500 *Rate:* 5.75% *Loan Term:* 4 years. Calculate the monthly payment.

7 *Car loan amount:* $30,000 *Rate:* 3.75% *Loan Term:* 6 years. Calculate the monthly payment.

8 *Car loan amount:* $25,500 *Rate:* 4.8% *Loan Term:* 5 years. Calculate the monthly payment.

9 Amy took out a student loan. *Loan Amount:* $14,000 *Rate:* 6.5% Loan Term: 3 years. Calculate the monthly payment

10 Ibrahim took out a student loan. *Loan Amount:* $32,500 *Rate:* 4.2% *Loan Term:* 4 years. Calculate his monthly payment.

11 Johanna decides to take out a student loan. *Loan Amount:* $9,800 *Rate:* 5.25% *Loan Term:* 2 years. Calculate her monthly payment.

12 You decide to take out a student loan. *Loan Amount:* $22,000 *Rate:* 6.1% *Loan Term:* 5 years. Calculate your monthly payment.

13 Aisha needs to get a student loan. *Loan Amount:* $18,500 *Rate:* 4.9% *Loan Term:* 4 years. Calculate her monthly payment.

14 I am thinking of getting a student loan. *Loan Amount:* $12,700 *Rate:* 5.75% *Loan Term:* 3 years. What will my monthly payment be?

15 *Car Loan Amount:* $21,000 *Rate:* 4.25% *Loan Term:* 5 years. Calculate the monthly payment.

16 *Student Loan Amount:* $15,200 *Rate:* 3.9% *Loan Term:* 4 years. Calculate the monthly payment.

17 *Car Loan Amount:* $10,600 *Rate:* 4.6% *Loan Term:* 3 years. Calculate the monthly payment.

18 *Student Loan Amount:* $15,000 *Rate:* 6.2% *Loan Term:* 5 years. Calculate the monthly payment.

19 *Student Loan Amount:* $25,000 *Rate:* 4.8% *Loan Term:* 7 years. Calculate the monthly payment.

20 *Student Loan Amount:* $12,500 *Rate:* 3.5% *Loan Term:* 3 years. Calculate the (a) monthly payment and (b) total interest paid on entire loan.

21 *Student Loan Amount:* $9,000 *Rate:* 4.2% *Loan Term:* 4 years. Calculate the (a) monthly payment and the (b) cost of borrowing (principal + interest) by end of term.

22 *Student Loan Amount:* $22,500 *Rate:* 5.1% *Loan Term:* 6 years. Calculate the (a) monthly payment and (b) total interest paid on entire loan.

(i) Amortization Schedule

An amortization schedule is a detailed table that outlines the repayment of a loan over time. It breaks down each payment into its principal and interest components, showing how the loan balance decreases as payments are made. Amortization schedules are commonly used for mortgages, car loans, and other installment loans where regular payments are made over the course of the loan term.

The key components of an amortization schedule include:

Payment Number: The sequential number of the payment.

Payment Amount: The total payment amount that needs to be made in each period, including principal and interest portions.

Principal Payment: The portion of the payment that goes towards reducing the loan's principal amount.

Interest Payment: The portion of the payment that covers the interest charged on the remaining loan balance.

Total payment: The sum of the principal payment and the interest payment.

Remaining Principal/Balance: The outstanding loan balance after each payment is made. It decreases as the loan is paid off.

By the end of the loan term, all principal and interest should be paid off, ending with a zero balance.

Let's create an amortization schedule based on the following scenario:

You want to get a loan for $100,000. The bank offers you an interest rate of 1.79% per year for a term of 12 months. Create an amortization schedule for your payments, assuming fixed monthly payments.

Calculate the monthly payment using the amortization formula.

UNIT 10

Mortgages

Calculating mortgages is a crucial skill in financial literacy that can empower you to make informed decisions when purchasing or refinancing a home. Understanding the intricacies of mortgage calculations enables you to determine affordability, compare loan options, and plan your finances effectively. It allows you to learn how to assess your financial situation, considering income, expenses, and debt-to-income ratio to determine how much of a mortgage you can afford. By comparing different mortgage options, you can analyze interest rates, loan terms, and down payment requirements to make reasonable decisions. Calculating mortgage payments also allows you to include them in your monthly budgets and plan your overall financial goals effectively.

Key Concepts

- Principal: The initial loan amount borrowed to purchase a home.

- Interest Rate: The annual percentage rate charged by the lender for borrowing the funds.

- Loan Term: The duration of the mortgage, typically expressed in years.

- Down Payment: The initial payment made by the borrower, reducing the principal amount.

- Amortization: The process of gradually paying off the mortgage through regular payments.

- Monthly Payment: The amount to be paid by the borrower each month, comprising principal and interest.

- Total Interest Paid: The cumulative interest paid over the entire loan term.

10.1 Mortgage Payments

The formula for calculating mortgage payments is based on the concept of amortization, which involves spreading out the repayment of a loan over a specific period of time, the same for-mula we used in the loan amortization section.

$$M = P \times (r \times (1 + r)^n) / ((1 + r)^n - 1)$$

Where:

M = Monthly mortgage payment

P = Principal loan amount (the initial amount borrowed)

r = Monthly interest rate (annual interest rate divided by 12 months)

n = Total number of monthly payments (loan term in months)

Let's break down the formula step by step:

Step 1: Calculate the monthly interest rate. To determine the monthly interest rate, divide the annual interest rate by 12 to convert it to a monthly rate. For example, if the annual inter-est rate is 5%, the monthly interest rate would be 0.05/12 = 0.004167.

Step 2: Calculate the total number of monthly payments. To calculate the total number of monthly payments, multiply the number of years in the loan term by 12. For example, if the loan term is 25 years, the total number of monthly payments would be 25 x 12 = 300.

Step 3: Calculate the monthly mortgage payment. Using the values obtained from steps 1 and 2, plug them into the formula:

$$M = P \times (r \times (1 + r)^n) / ((1 + r)^n - 1)$$

This formula takes into account the loan amount, interest rate, and loan term to determine the fixed monthly payment required to fully repay the mortgage over the specified period.

By substituting the values for P, r, and n into the formula, you can calculate the monthly mortgage payment.

It is important to note that this formula assumes a fixed interest rate for the entire loan term. In the case of adjustable-rate mortgages where the interest rate can change or vary over time, the formula may differ or additional calculations may be required to account for rate adjustments. Additionally, the formula does not account for other costs associated with homeownership, such as property taxes and insurance which may be applicable in certain cases.

Let's calculate monthly mortgage payments. The first one has been solved for you.

1 Shahad takes out a mortgage loan of $300,000 at an annual interest rate of 4.5%. The loan term is 25 years. Calculate her monthly mortgage payment.

SOLUTION

$$M = \$300{,}000 \times \frac{(0.00375 \times (1 + 0.00375)^{300})}{((1 + 0.00375)^{300} - 1)}$$

Calculate $(1 + 0.00375)^{300}$ and $((1 + 0.00375)^{300} - 1)$ separately.

$(1 + 0.00375)^{300} = 3.073742528$

$((1 + 0.00375)^{300} - 1) = 2.073742528$

Monthly payment = $300,000 × (0.00375 × 3.073742528)/ 2.073742528

Monthly payment = $1,667.50

2 If you take out a 25 year mortgage loan in the amount of $300,000 with a monthly payment of $1,667.50, what is the (a) total cost of borrowing (principal + interest) and (b) total interest paid?

3 You are purchasing a house for $500,000. You have saved $100,000 for a down payment. What percentage of the purchase price is the down payment?

4 You want to purchase a house for $400,000. You have saved $80,000 for a down payment. What is the mortgage loan amount that you require?

5 You are purchasing a house for $250,000. The bank requires a down payment of 20%. How much is the down payment?

6 You are purchasing a house for $350,000. You have saved $70,000 as a down payment. What percentage of the purchase price is the down payment?

7 Determine the total number of monthly payments for a 30-year mortgage.

8 A homeowner has a mortgage loan of $250,000 with an annual interest rate of 4%, and a mortgage term of 3 years. Calculate the monthly mortgage payment.

9 Mark has a mortgage loan of $400,000 with an annual interest rate of 3.5% and a 12 year term. Estimate the annual interest paid within the first 12 months.

10 Kawar has a mortgage loan of $150,000 with an annual interest rate of 5.25% over a 25 year term. Calculate his monthly interest paid during the first year.

11 Yunus has a mortgage loan of $350,000 with an annual interest rate of 4% and a term of 15 years. Calculate his monthly mortgage payment.

12 Tolga secures a mortgage loan of $250,000 at an annual interest rate of 3.75%. The loan term is 30 years. What is the total of mortgage payments at the end of the first year?

13 A homeowner takes out a mortgage loan of $400,000 at an annual interest rate of 5%. The loan term is 20 years. Calculate the monthly mortgage payment.

14 A homeowner takes out a mortgage loan of $500,000 at an annual interest rate of 4.25%. The loan term is 15 years. Calculate the monthly mortgage payment.

15 Barry secures a mortgage loan of $350,000 at an annual interest rate of 7%. The loan term is 20 years. How much interest does he pay per month the first year?

16 Pique takes out a mortgage loan of $400,000 at an annual interest rate of 5%. The loan term is 30 years. Calculate the total amount of interest Pique will pay for the entire term of the mortgage.

17 Talal wants to buy a house for $175,000. He has to pay a down payment of 15% and decides to get a mortgage for the remaining balance at an annual interest rate of 8% for 25 years. What is the total cost of borrowing (principal + interest)?

18 Shazia's monthly mortgage payment on her townhouse is $965.23. She also has to pay annual property tax of $2,356. How much mortgage and property tax must Shazia pay per month?

19 Mikey has a home valued at $1,900,000. Property tax in his district is charged at an annual rate of 7% of the value of property. How much property tax does Mikey have to pay?

Purchasing Power

Purchasing power is the amount of goods and services that can be purchased with a unit of currency.

Purchasing power can weaken over time due to inflation. Inflation is the general increase in prices of goods and services over time, resulting in the erosion of the value of currency. This is because rising prices effectively decrease the number of goods or services you can buy. Purchasing power is also known as a currency's buying power. One U.S. measure of purchasing power is the Consumer Price Index, which measures the overall change in the prices of goods and services that people typically buy over time. Central banks adjust interest rates to try to keep prices stable and maintain purchasing power.

Exponential decay in purchasing power refers to the decline in the value or buying power of money over time due to the impact of inflation. Exponential decay implies that the decline in purchasing power is not linear but follows an exponential or compounding pattern. This means that the rate at which the value of money decreases, accelerates over time. As prices rise, each unit of currency can purchase fewer goods and services, leading to a decrease in the overall purchasing power.

For example, suppose you have $100 today, and the inflation rate is 3% per year. After one year, the purchasing power of that $100 will decline by 3%, leaving you with the equivalent purchasing power of $97. In the following year, the same 3% decline applies to $97, resulting in a further decrease to $94.09, and so on. Over time, the purchasing power diminishes at an increasing rate due to the compounding effect of inflation.

Exponential decay in purchasing power highlights the importance of considering inflation when making financial decisions and long-term financial planning. It emphasizes the need to account for inflation in budgeting, investment strategies, retirement planning, and setting financial goals to preserve and grow wealth effectively over time.

Conversely, exponential growth portrays the compounding increase of an investment or asset's value. As time progresses, the growth rate leads to substantial gains fueled by the reinvestment of returns.

11.1 Exponential Decay

To calculate exponential decay in purchasing power, we use the following formula:

$$f(x) = a(1 - r)^t$$

f(x): the value of money at a future time after experiencing inflation.

a: the initial value of money

r: the rate at which the value of money is decreasing each year due to inflation, expressed as a decimal.

t: the time period or time factor over which the inflation occurs.

The first one has been solved for you.

1   The inflation rate in a country is 4% per year. What will be the purchasing power of $1,000 be after 10 years?

SOLUTION

Calculate the inflation-adjusted purchasing power after 10 years.

Apply exponential decay formula: $f(x) = a(1 - r)^t$

$f(x) = \$1,000 \times (1 - 0.04)^{10}$

$f(x) = \$1,000 \times (0.664832636)$

$f(x) = \$664.83$

Therefore, the purchasing power of $1,000 after 10 years will be $664.83.

2 If the annual inflation rate is 6%, what will the purchasing power of $1,000 be after 9 years?

3 The inflation rate is 1.5% per year. What will the purchasing power of $500 be after 8 years?

4 The purchasing power of a currency decreases by 5% each year. If $1,000 is invested today, what will its purchasing power be after 10 years?

5 The purchasing power of a currency decreases by 4.5% each year. If $10,000 is invested today, what will its purchasing power be after 15 years?

6 Suppose the purchasing power of currency decreases by 5% annually. If the price of a bottle of shampoo is $10 and you have a budget of $100 to spend on shampoo, how many bottles of shampoo can you buy (a) after 1 year? (b) after 2 years? (c) after 3 years? (d) after 8 years?

11.2 Exponential Growth

To calculate exponential growth, use the following formula:

$$f(x) = a(1 + r)^t$$

1 Your company is currently valued at $5,000 and is projected to grow in value at a rate of 7% annually. If you plan to sell the business in 15 years, how much will your business be worth at that time based on this projection?

2 Mary invests 200,000 rupees in mutual funds that offer an annual growth rate of 5%. How much will her investment be worth in 10 years based on this information?

3 Rushee's painting is currently valued at 1,500 Euros and is expected to increase in value at a rate of 2% annually. Based on this information, how much will the painting be worth in 16 years?

4   The purchasing power of a currency increases by 5% each year. If $1,000 is invested today, what will its purchasing power be after 10 years?

5   Imagine you have $100 and the price of a bottle of shampoo is $10. The annual rate of deflation is 10%. How many bottles of shampoo can you purchase (a) after 1 year? (b) after 2 years? (c) after 3 years? (d) after 8 years?

Capital Appreciation and Capital Depreciation

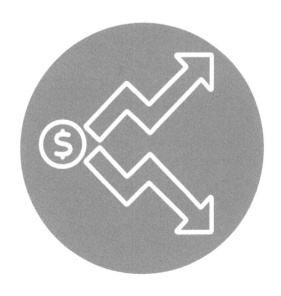

12.1 Capital Appreciation

Capital appreciation refers to an increase in the value of an asset over time. It occurs when the market price or fair value of an asset rises, resulting in a higher worth or valuation than its initial purchase price. Capital appreciation is commonly associated with investments in assets such as stocks, real estate, and financial securities.

When an asset appreciates in value, the difference between the current market value and the initial purchase price represents the capital appreciation. It is an important concept in investment and finance as it measures the potential returns and growth of an asset.

Investors and individuals track capital appreciation to assess the performance of their investments and make informed decisions regarding buying, selling, or holding assets. It is an essential factor in evaluating the overall profitability and growth potential of an investment portfolio or specific assets.

Capital appreciation can be calculated using the following formulas:

Capital Appreciation (Dollar Amount):

Current Market Value-Initial Purchase Price

Capital Appreciation (Percentage/Rate):

$$\frac{Current\ Market\ Value - Initial\ Purchase\ Price}{Initial\ Purchase\ Price} \times 100$$

Let's try some questions by applying the capital appreciation formula.

1   You purchased a stock for $50 per share, and after one year, the stock price increased to $65 per share. What is the percentage of capital appreciation?

2   You bought a house for $200,000, and after three years, the house value rose to $250,000. What is the percentage of capital appreciation?

3   You invested $10,000 in a mutual fund, and after five years, your investment grew to $15,000. What is the percentage of capital appreciation?

4   You purchased a piece of artwork for $2,500, and a few years later, its value increased to $3,800. What is the percentage of capital appreciation?

5   You acquired 100 shares of a company's stock for $20 per share, and after two years, the stock price rose to $30 per share. What is the percentage of capital appreciation?

6   You invested $5,000 in a real estate property, and over five years, its value increased to $7,500. What is the percentage of capital appreciation?

7   You purchased a vintage car for $30,000, and after three years, its value went up to $45,000. What is the percentage of capital appreciation?

8   You invested $1,000 in a cryptocurrency, and after six months, its value increased to $2,500. What is the percentage of capital appreciation?

9   You bought a piece of land for $50,000, and over seven years, its value appreciated to $80,000. What is the percentage of capital appreciation?

10 You acquired 500 shares of a company's stock for $10 per share, and after four years, the stock price increased to $25 per share. What is the percentage of capital appreciation?

12.2 Capital Depreciation

Capital depreciation refers to the decrease in value or the wear and tear of an asset over time. It represents the expense incurred by a business as a result of the reduction in the asset's value. Depreciation is an important concept in accounting and finance as it allows businesses to allocate the cost of an asset over its useful life, reflecting the gradual loss of value due to factors such as obsolescence, wear and tear, or technological advancements.

Straight-Line Depreciation Method

The most commonly used formula to calculate capital depreciation is the straight-line depreciation method. The formula for straight-line depreciation is as follows:

Depreciation Expense = (*Initial Cost – Salvage Value*)/ *Useful Life*

- **Initial Cost:** This refers to the original cost or purchase price of the asset.

- **Salvage Value:** Also known as residual value or scrap value, it represents the estimated value of the asset at the end of its useful life.

- **Useful Life:** This is the estimated lifespan or duration over which the asset is expected to be used by the business before it becomes obsolete or has no economic value.

The formula subtracts the salvage value from the cost of the asset to determine the depreciable base, which is the amount that will be spread over the useful life of the asset. The depreciable base is then divided by the useful life to calculate the annual depreciation expense.

It's worth noting that there are other depreciation methods as well, such as the double-declining balance method, sum-of-years-digits method and units-of-production method. These methods may have different formulas and approaches to calculate depreciation based on factors such as accelerated depreciation, varying rates or production output.

The first question has been solved for you.

1   Initial Cost = $10,000

Salvage Value = $2,000

Useful Life = 5 years.

What is the depreciation expense each year using the annual straight-line formula?

SOLUTION

Depreciation Expense = ($10,000 - $2,000)/5

Depreciation Expense = $8,000/5

Depreciation Expense = $1,600 per year

2   A car was purchased for $30,000. If it has a useful life of 10 years and a salvage value of $5,000, calculate the annual straight-line depreciation.

3   A computer was purchased for $2,000. After 3 years, it is expected to have a salvage value of $500. Calculate the annual straight-line depreciation.

4   A building was purchased for $500,000. It has a useful life of 40 years and is expected to have a salvage value of $50,000. Calculate the annual straight-line depreciation.

5   A company purchases machinery for $100,000. It has a useful life of 5 years and is expected to have no salvage value. Calculate the annual straight-line depreciation.

6   A company purchased equipment for $80,000. It has a useful life of 8 years and is expected to have a salvage value of $5,000. Calculate the annual straight-line depreciation.

7   Marissa bought an office space for $450,000 and one year later its current value was $340,000. Calculate the rate of depreciation as a percentage.

8   Carlos purchases a motorcycle for $26,700. It has a salvage value of $2,500 and a useful life of 5 years. Calculate the (a) annual depreciation expense, (b) the percentage of capital depreciation and (c) the annual rate of depreciation as a percentage?

9   Stanos purchases a laptop for $1,500. It is expected to have a useful life of 4 years and a salvage value of $200. Calculate the book value of the laptop after 3 years using the straight-line method.

10 Marcos purchases a mattress for $458. It is expected to have a useful life of 5 years and a salvage value of $80. (a) Calculate the book value of the mattress after 2 years using the straight-line method.

11 **Declining Balance Method**

A company buys a piece of machinery for $80,000. The machinery has a useful life of 10 years and a salvage value of $5,000. Calculate the book value and annual depreciation for year 1 and year 2 using the straight-line method. (b) Calculate the book value for year 1 and year 2 using the declining balance method with a depreciation rate of 20% per year.

In the **declining balance method**, the depreciation rate is applied to the remaining book value each year using this formula:

Initial value × *Depreciation rate*

12 **Sum of the Years' Digits:**

A business purchases a delivery truck for $50,000. The truck is expected to have a useful life of 6 years and zero salvage value. Calculate the annual depreciation for years 1, 2 and 3 using the sum-of-the-years' digits (SYD) method.

In the **SYD method**, the annual depreciation is determined based on the sum of the years of useful life.

- Calculate the SYD

  $SYD = n \times \left(\dfrac{n+1}{2}\right)$ *where n is the useful life of the asset*

- Then, calculate the annual depreciation expense

  Annual depreciation expense:

  (*Years remaining/SYD*) *x* (*Initial value – Salvage value*)

UNIT 13

Insurance

You have probably heard about insurance before. It involves a financial arrangement in which individuals or entities transfer the risk of potential loss or damage to an insurance company in exchange for regular premium payments. The insuranoc company, in turn, provides financial compensation or coverage in the event of specified incidents or losses.

Some common types of insurance include:

- Health Insurance: Provides coverage for medical expenses.

- Auto Insurance: Protects against financial loss due to accidents, theft or damage to vehicles.

- Homeowners/Renters Insurance: Offers coverage for property damage or theft.

- Life Insurance: Provides financial support to beneficiaries in the event of the insured person's death.

- Property Insurance: Protects individuals or businesses against claims for bodily injury or property damage caused to others.

Try calculating the insurance premiums in the following questions.

1 An auto insurance policy has a deductible of $500 and a premium rate of 5% of the car's value. If the car's value is $20,000, what is the annual premium?

2 A homeowner's insurance policy charges an annual premium of 0.3% of the insured value of the house. If a house is insured for $300,000, what is the annual premium?

3 A health insurance policy has a monthly premium rate of $200 per person. If a family of four is covered by the policy, what is their monthly premium?

4 A life insurance policy charges a premium of $10 per $1,000 of coverage. If the policy provides a coverage of $100,000, what is the annual premium?

5   An insurance policy for a business charges a premium rate of 2% of the total insured value of the company's assets. If the total insured value is $1,500,000, what is the annual premium?

6   A travel insurance policy charges a premium of $20 per person per week of coverage. If a family of three is traveling for two weeks, what is their total premium?

7   An insurance policy for a commercial vehicle charges a premium rate of $0.10 per mile driven. If the vehicle is driven 10,000 miles in a year, what is the annual premium?

8   A pet insurance policy charges a monthly premium of $50 for cats and $70 for dogs. If a household has two cats and one dog, what is their monthly premium?

9   A disability insurance policy charges a monthly premium of $1.50 per $100 of coverage. If a person has a total coverage of $200,000, what is their monthly premium?

10 A motorcycle insurance policy charges a premium rate of 8% of the motorcycle's value. If a motorcycle is valued at $8,000, what is the annual premium?

11 A homeowner's insurance policy charges a premium of 0.2% of the insured value of the contents of the house. If the contents are insured for $50,000, what is the annual premium?

12 life insurance policy charges a premium of $20 per $1,000 of coverage. If the policy provides a coverage of $500,000, what is the annual premium?

13 An insurance policy for a business charges a premium rate of 1.5% of the company's annual revenue. If the company's revenue is $2,000,000, what is the annual premium?

14 A travel insurance policy charges a premium of $10 per person per day of coverage. If a group of five people is traveling for seven days, what is their total premium?

15 An insurance policy for a commercial vehicle charges a premium rate of $0.25 per mile driven. If the vehicle is driven 20,000 miles in a year, what is the annual premium?

16 A pet insurance policy charges a monthly premium of $40 for cats and $60 for dogs. If a household has three cats and two dogs, what is their monthly premium?

17 A disability insurance policy charges a premium of $2 per $100 of coverage per month. If a person has coverage of $300,000, what is their monthly premium?

18 A motorcycle insurance policy charges a premium rate of 10% of the motorcycle's value. If a motorcycle is valued at $5,000, what is the annual premium?

19 A homeowner's insurance policy charges a premium of 0.25% of the insured value of the house. If a house is insured for $400,000, what is the annual premium?

20 A life insurance policy charges a premium of $15 per $1,000 of coverage. If the policy provides a coverage of $250,000, what is the annual premium?

Retirement Planning

While retirement may seem distant, the decisions you make today will shape the quality of your future. Let's dive into some key concepts of retirement planning to understand how to secure a comfortable retirement.

14.1 Saving Early and the Power of Compounding

We learned about the future value of investments earlier in the course. The scenarios we explored involved lump sum investments earning simple or compound interest over a specific period of time. Now, we will learn how to calculate the future value of an investment made through regular deposits within a specific period of time.

We will use the following future value formula when making regular deposits into savings:

$$FV = P \times (1 + r)^{nt} - 1$$

Where:

FV = future value of the savings

P = periodic deposit amount

r = interest rate per period expressed as a decimal

n = number of compounding periods per year

t = number of years

Please keep in mind that the formula assumes that the deposits are made at the end of each compounding period and that the interest is compounded on a regular basis.

Let's try a few questions.

1   If Jane starts saving $300 per month at an annual interest rate of 6%, compounded monthly, at age 30 and plans to retire at age 65, how much will she have accumulated by the time she retires?

2   What if Mathew starts saving $300 per month at an annual interest rate of 6%, compounded monthly, at the age of 50 and plans to retire at 65? What would the value of his savings be by the time he retires?

3   If Mahmoud starts saving 100 AED per month at the age of 18 until he retires at the age of 65, what would the value of his savings be by the time he retires if his investment earns an annual interest of 5%, compounded monthly?

4   If Shahida starts saving 100 AED per month at the age of 45 until she retires at the age of 65, what would the value of her savings be by the time she retires if her investment earns an annual interest of 5%, compounded monthly?

14.2 Estimate Retirement Needs - the "70 - 80% rule"

When estimating your expenses, including housing, healthcare, travel and leisure activities during retirement, a common rule of thumb is the "70 - 80% rule," where you aim to replace 70 - 80% of your pre-retirement income to maintain your standard of living.

Let's apply this rule to the following scenarios.

1   Assume your current annual income is $60,000 and you aim to replace 75% of it during retirement, how much should you plan for annually during retirement?

2   Maha's current annual income is GBP 80,000. According to the 70 -80% rule how much should she aim to have annually during retirement if she plans to replace 70% of her pre-retirement income?

3   Isabelle earns an annual income of 100,000 Euros. She plans to replace 76% of her pre-retirement income when she retires. How much should she plan to have annually during retirement?

4   Arjun earns 500,000 Rupees and wants to replace 80% of his pre-retirement income during retirement. How much should he plan to have annually during retirement?

14.3 Investment Strategy: Balancing Risk and Returns

Balancing risk and returns is a crucial consideration when planning for retirement. It involves making investment decisions that optimize the potential for higher returns while managing the associated risks. Let's explore this concept further:

- Risk Tolerance: As you approach retirement, your risk tolerance tends to decrease. This is because you have less time to recover from market downturns. While stocks historically offer higher returns, they are also more volatile. Bonds, on the other hand, are generally more stable but offer lower returns. Balancing your portfolio between these asset classes is essential.

- Diversification: Diversifying your investments across different asset classes (stocks, bonds, real estate, etc.) can help reduce risk. If one asset class underperforms, others may provide stability.

- Age and Time Horizon: Your age plays a significant role in determining your risk tolerance. Younger individuals have more time to recover from market fluctuations, allowing them to take on higher-risk investments. As you near retirement, consider shifting towards more conservative investments.

Let's consider two hypothetical portfolios for individuals with different risk appetites:

Aggressive Portfolio

- Allocation: 80% stocks, 20% bonds
- Expected Annual Returns: Stocks (10%), Bonds (4%)
- Expected Average Portfolio Return:
- (0.80×0.10)+(0.20×0.04) = 0.08 + 0.008 = 0.088 = 8.8%

Conservative Portfolio

- Allocation: 40% stocks, 60% bonds
- Expected Annual Returns: Stocks (7%), Bonds (3%)
- Expected Average Portfolio Return:
- (0.40 × 0.07) + (0.60 × 0.03) = 0.028 + 0.0.018 = 0.046 = 4.6%

In this example, the aggressive portfolio offers higher expected returns (8.8%) compared to the conservative portfolio (4.4%). However, the aggressive portfolio also comes with higher volatility, which could lead to more significant losses during market downturns.

Balancing risk and returns involves finding a mix that aligns with your risk tolerance and financial goals. A balanced approach helps you achieve growth while safeguarding your retirement nest egg from excessive volatility.

UNIT 15

Business

15.1 Types of Businesses

When it comes to starting a business, there are various structures to consider, each with its own advantages and disadvantages. Let's explore three common types of businesses: sole proprietorships, partnerships, and corporations.

1   Sole Proprietorships

Pros

- Simplicity: A sole proprietorships is usually the easiest and most straightforward type of business to set up. It involves a single owner who has full control over decision-making.

- Direct Profits: The owner receives all the profits generated by the business.

- Minimal Regulations: Sole proprietorships usually have fewer legal requirements and regulations to follow.

Cons

- Limited Resources: Funding and resources are limited to the owner's personal savings or loans.

- Unlimited Liability: The owner is personally responsible for all the business's debts and liabilities.

- Limited Expertise: The owner may lack expertise in certain areas required for the business's growth.

2   Partnerships

Pros

- Shared Responsibilities: Partners can share the workload, skills, and resources, allowing for better decision-making.

- Diverse Expertise: Partners bring different skills and expertise to the table, which can enhance the business's overall operations.

- Shared Financial Burden: Partners can pool their resources and investments for business growth.

Cons

- Conflict Potential: Disagreements between partners can arise, affecting decision-making and potentially harming the business.
- Shared Profits: Profits are divided among partners, potentially leading to less individual earnings.
- Joint Liability: Each partner is liable for the actions and debts of the other partners.

3   Corporations

Pros

- Limited Liability: Shareholders' personal assets are protected from business liabilities.
- Access to Capital: Corporations can raise funds by issuing stocks to investors.
- Professional Management: Corporations can attract professional managers to run the business efficiently.

Cons

- Complex Setup: Corporations involve complex legal and administrative procedures for formation and operation.
- Double Taxation: Corporations are subject to taxation at both the corporate level and the individual shareholder level.
- Regulatory Requirements: Corporations have stricter regulatory and reporting obligations.

Remember, the choice of business structure should align with your goals, resources, and risk tolerance. Each type offers different benefits and challenges, so it's essential to carefully consider your options before launching your entrepreneurial journey.

15.2 Financial Documents and Business Expenses

The financial statements of a company record important financial data on every aspect of a business's activities. Companies use the balance sheet, income statement and cash flow statement to manage the operations of their business. The income statement provides an overview of the company's financial performance, showcasing its revenue, expenses, and resulting net income (profit) for a specific period.

a. The Income Statement

Here's an example of an income statement:

Income Statement for XYZ Company For the Year Ended December 31, 20XX

Revenue

Sales Revenue $500,000

Other Revenue $10,000

Total Revenue $510,000

Expenses

Cost of Goods Sold $250,000

Operating Expenses

- Salaries and Wages $100,000
- Rent $25,000
- Utilities $10,000
- Advertising $15,000
- Depreciation $20,000
- Other Expenses $5,000

Total Operating Expenses: $175,000

Interest Expense $5,000

Income Tax Expense $50,000

Net Income: (Profit) $30,000

In the income statement above, the various components are as follows:

- **Revenue:** This section represents the company's income generated from sales and other sources. In this example, sales revenue is $500,000, and other revenue (such as interest income or rental income) is $10,000. The total revenue is calculated as the sum of sales revenue and other revenue, which equals $510,000.

- **Expenses:** This section lists the various expenses incurred by the company during the year. Cost of Goods Sold (COGS) represents the expenses directly related to producing the goods or services sold, which is $250,000 in this case. Operating expenses include salaries and wages, rent, utilities, advertising, depreciation, and other expenses, totaling $175,000. Interest expense represents the interest paid on loans or credit, which amounts to $5,000. Income tax expense denotes the taxes owed on the company's taxable income and is $50,000 in this example.

- **Net Income (Profit):** Net income is the final line item on the income statement and represents the company's profit after deducting all expenses from the revenue. It is calculated by subtracting the total expenses (including cost of goods sold, operating expenses, interest expense, and income tax expense) from the total revenue. In this case, the net income (profit) is $30,000.

b. The Balance Sheet

The balance sheet provides a snapshot of a company's financial position at a specific point in time, showcasing its assets, liabilities, and shareholders' equity.

Here's an example of a balance sheet:

Balance Sheet of XYZ Company As of December 31, 20XX

Assets: Current Assets

- Cash and Cash Equivalents $50,000
- Accounts Receivable $40,000
- Inventory $60,000
- Prepaid Expenses $5,000 Total Current Assets $155,000

Fixed Assets

- Property, Plant, and Equipment $200,000
- Less: Accumulated Depreciation ($50,000) Net Fixed Assets $150,000

Total Assets $305,000

Liabilities and Shareholders' Equity: Liabilities: Current Liabilities

- Accounts Payable $25,000
- Short-Term Loans $15,000
- Accrued Expenses $10,000

Total Current Liabilities $50,000

Long-Term Liabilities

- Long-Term Loans $100,000

Total Liabilities $150,000

Shareholders' Equity

- Common Stock $100,000
- Retained Earnings $55,000

Total Shareholders' Equity $155,000

Total Liabilities and Shareholders' Equity: $305,000

In the balance sheet above, the various components are as follows:

- **Assets:** This section represents what the company owns or has a claim to. It is divided into current assets and fixed assets. Current assets include cash and cash equivalents, accounts receivable, inventory, and prepaid expenses, totaling $155,000. Fixed assets include property, plant, and equipment, with a net value of $150,000 (after deducting accumulated depreciation).

- **Liabilities:** This section represents what the company owes to others. It is divided into current liabilities and long-term liabilities. Current liabilities include accounts payable, short-term loans, and accrued expenses, totaling $50,000. Long-term liabilities represent long-term loans amounting to $100,000.

- **Shareholders' Equity:** This section represents the owners' claims to the company's assets. It includes common stock and retained earnings. Common stock represents the amount invested by shareholders, which is $100,000. Retained earnings represent the accumulated profits of the company, totaling $55,000.

- **Total Liabilities and Shareholders' Equity:** This is the sum of the liabilities and shareholders' equity sections and represents the total value of the company's financing, which in this case is $305,000.

c. The Cash Flow Statement

The cash flow statement provides an overview of the company's cash flows from operating, investing and financing activities. A cash flow statement typically includes three main components:

1 Operating activities

2 Investing activities

3 Financial activities

Here is an example of a Cash Flow Statement:

XYZ Company

Cash Flow Statement

For the Year Ended December 31, 2022

Operating Activities

Net Income: $100,000

Adjustments for non-cash items:

Depreciation Expenses: $20,000

Loss on Sale of Equipment: $5,000

Changes in working capital:

Increase in Accounts Receivable: ($15,000)

Decrease in Inventory: $10,000

Increase in Accounts Payable: $8,000

Net Cash Provided by Operating Activities: $118,000

Investing Activities

Purchase of Equipment: ($50,000)

Sale of Marketable Securities: $30,000

Net Cash Used in Investing Activities: ($20,000)

Financing Activities

Proceeds from Issuance of Common Stock: $40,000

Payment of Dividends: ($20,000)

Net Cash Provided by Financing Activities: $20,000

Net Increase in Cash: $118,000 - $20,000 + $20,000 = $118,000

Cash in Beginning of Year: $50,000

Cash at End of Year: $50,000 + $118,000 = $168,000

Now try solving these questions as they relate to typical items found in business financial documents.

Cost of Goods Sold (COGS)

Use the following formula to calculate the COGS.

Beginning inventory + purchases of inventory – ending inventory = COGS

1 A retail store has the following information for a particular month:

- Beginning inventory: $10,000

- Purchases during the month: $5,000

- Ending inventory: $8,000

Calculate the Cost of Goods Sold (COGS) for the month.

2 A clothing store purchased $40,000 worth of inventory at the beginning of the year. During the year, they made additional purchases totaling $20,000. The ending inventory was $15,000. Calculate the cost of goods sold for the clothing store.

3 A manufacturing company had raw material inventory worth $30,000 at the beginning of the year. They purchased additional raw materials worth $50,000 during the year. The ending raw material inventory was $25,000. Calculate the cost of goods sold for the manufacturing company.

4 A restaurant purchased food and beverages worth $15,000 at the beginning of the month. Throughout the month, they made additional purchases totaling $8,000. The ending inventory of food and beverages was $6,000. Calculate the cost of goods sold for the restaurant.

5 An electronics store had inventory worth $60,000 at the beginning of the quarter. They made additional purchases of electronics products worth $25,000 during the quarter. The ending inventory was $40,000. Calculate the cost of goods sold for the electronics store.

6 A bakery purchased baking ingredients worth $10,000 at the beginning of the year. They made additional purchases

of ingredients totaling $5,000 during the year. The ending inventory of baking ingredients was $8,000. Calculate the cost of goods sold for the bakery.

7   A bookstore had a beginning inventory of $10,000. During the year, they made purchases totaling $20,000. The ending inventory was valued at $8,000. Calculate the cost of goods sold for the bookstore.

8   A grocery store had a beginning inventory of $50,000. They made additional purchases totaling $30,000 throughout the month. The ending inventory was valued at $40,000. Calculate the cost of goods sold for the grocery store.

Gross Profit Margin

Use the following formula to calculate gross profit margin.

$$\frac{(Sales - COGS)}{Sales} \times 100$$

1   A retailer has total sales of $800,000 and the cost of goods sold is $600,000. Calculate the gross profit margin for the retailer.

2   A software company has total revenue of $1,200,000 and the cost of sales is $800,000. Calculate the gross profit margin for the software company.

3   A restaurant has total food and beverage sales of $400,000 and the cost of goods sold is $200,000. Calculate the gross profit margin for the restaurant.

4   A manufacturing company has total revenue of $2,000,000 and the cost of goods manufactured is $1,200,000. Calculate the gross profit margin for the manufacturing company.

5   A consulting firm has total sales of $300,000 and the direct costs related to providing services amount to $100,000. Calculate the gross profit margin for the consulting firm.

6   A grocery store has total sales of $1,000,000 and the cost of goods sold is $700,000. Calculate the gross profit margin for the grocery store.

Net Income

Use the following formula to calculate net income.

Revenue – COGS – Expenses

1   A small retail business had total revenues of $50,000 in a year. The cost of goods sold was $25,000, and operating expenses were $12,000. Calculate the net income for the business.

2   An online consulting firm generated total sales of $100,000 in a year. The cost of services provided was $35,000, and the company incurred operating expenses of $20,000. Calculate the net income for the consulting firm.

3   A manufacturing company had total revenue of $500,000 in a year. The cost of goods manufactured was $250,000, and operating expenses were $150,000. The company also received a non-operating income of $25,000. Calculate the net income for the manufacturing company.

4   A restaurant recorded total sales of $200,000 in a year. The cost of food and beverages sold was $80,000, and operating expenses amounted to $60,000. The restaurant also received a non-operating expense of $5,000. Calculate the net income for the restaurant.

5   A software company generated total revenue of $1,000,000 in a year. The cost of software development was $500,000, and operating expenses were $300,000. The company also received interest income of $10,000. Calculate the net income for the software company.

6   A company has total revenue of $500,000, cost of goods sold of $300,000, and expenses of $150,000. Calculate the net income for the company.

7　A retail store has total revenue of $800,000, cost of goods sold of $600,000, and expenses of $200,000. Calculate the net income for the retail store.

8　A consulting firm has total revenue of $1,200,000, cost of goods sold of $0, and expenses of $800,000. Calculate the net income for the consulting firm.

9　A restaurant has total revenue of $400,000, cost of goods sold of $150,000, and expenses of $200,000. Calculate the net income for the restaurant.

10　A manufacturing company has total revenue of $2,000,000, cost of goods sold of $1,200,000, and expenses of $820,000. Calculate the net income for the manufacturing company.

11　A small business has total revenue of $300,000, cost of goods sold of $100,000, and expenses of $250,000. Calculate the net income for the small business.

12　An e-commerce store has total revenue of $1,000,000, cost of goods sold of $700,000, and expenses of $400,000. Calculate the net income for the e-commerce store.

Break-Even Point

Understanding your break even point allows you to know how many sales you need to make to cover your costs or make a profit. Any sales above the break-even point represent profit.

Use the following formula to calculate your break-even point.

Fixed costs/(sales price per unit – variable cost per unit)

1　A company has fixed costs of $50,000, a sales price per unit of $10, and a variable cost per unit of $6. Calculate the break-even point for the company.

2　A retail store has fixed costs of $100,000, a sales price per unit of $50, and a variable cost per unit of $30. Calculate the break-even point for the retail store.

3 A manufacturing company has fixed costs of $200,000, a sales price per unit of $100, and a variable cost per unit of $70. Calculate the break-even point for the manufacturing company.

4 A restaurant has fixed costs of $80,000, a sales price per unit of $20, and a variable cost per unit of $12. Calculate the break-even point for the restaurant.

5 A service-based business has fixed costs of $30,000, a sales price per unit of $100, and a variable cost per unit of $20. Calculate the break-even point for the service-based business.

6 A software company has fixed costs of $150,000, a sales price per unit of $200, and a variable cost per unit of $50. Calculate the break-even point for the software company.

7 A consulting firm has fixed costs of $50,000, a sales price per unit of $500, and a variable cost per unit of $200. Calculate the break-even point for the consulting firm.

Return on Investment

We covered the concept of ROI earlier in this course. Understanding ROI allows you to assess how much you have made from a business investment. Calculating return on investment can help you decide whether to continue investing in a particular activity.

Use the following formula to calculate return on investment.

((Amount generated - Cost of investment)/Cost of investment) x 100

1 An individual invests $10,000 in a stock and sells it later for $12,500. Calculate the return on investment for the individual.

2 A business invests $50,000 in marketing campaigns and generates an additional $100,000 in revenue. Calculate the return on investment for the business.

3   An individual invests $5,000 in a real estate property and sells it later for $6,500. Calculate the return on investment for the individual.

4   A company invests $100,000 in a new production facility and generates $150,000 in additional profits. Calculate the return on investment for the company.

5   An individual invests $20,000 in a startup and receives $30,000 in return. Calculate the return on investment for the individual.

Differentiating Fixed and Variable Costs

1   A manufacturing company has the following costs in a month:

- Rent: $2,000
- Raw Materials: $3,500
- Salaries: $5,000
- Property Tax: $600

Determine the fixed costs and variable costs for the company.

Calculating Monthly Payroll Expenses

1   Calculating Monthly Payroll Expenses A company has the following employee salaries for a month:

- Employee A: $3,500
- Employee B: $4,200
- Employee C: $2,800
- Employee D: $3,900

The company also pays its accountant a monthly salary of $5,500. Calculate the total monthly payroll expenses for the company.

Calculate total assets, total liabilities, and shareholders' equity

1   The following information is given for a company:

- Current Assets: $50,000

- Non-Current Assets: $100,000

- Current Liabilities: $30,000

- Long-Term Liabilities: $50,000

Calculate the total assets, total liabilities, and shareholders' equity for the company.

15.3 Entrepreneurship and Starting a New Business

Entrepreneurship refers to the process of starting, managing, and operating a business venture with the aim of creating and delivering value through innovative ideas, products, or services. Entrepreneurs play a vital role in driving economic growth and creating job opportunities.

From a financial perspective, entrepreneurs need to consider various costs and steps in order to launch and sustain their business. Here are some key financial aspects that entrepreneurs should consider:

- **Start-up Costs:** These include the initial expenses required to establish the business, such as market research, product development, legal fees, permits, licenses, office space, equipment, and inventory. Entrepreneurs need to estimate and secure the necessary funding to cover these costs.

- **Operational Costs:** These are ongoing expenses required to run the business on a day-to-day basis. Operational costs may include rent, utilities, salaries and wages, raw materials, marketing and advertising, insurance, and maintenance expenses.

It is crucial for entrepreneurs to carefully manage and budget for these costs to ensure the financial stability of the business.

- **Financing:** Entrepreneurs often need to secure financing to fund their business. They can consider various financing options, such as self-funding (using personal savings), loans from banks or financial institutions, angel investors, venture capital, crowdfunding, or government grants. Entrepreneurs need to assess the different sources of financing and determine the most suitable option based on their business needs and goals.

- **Revenue Generation:** Entrepreneurs must develop a clear revenue model to generate income and sustain their business. They need to identify their target market, determine pricing strategies, and create effective sales and marketing plans to attract customers and generate sales.

- **Cash Flow Management:** Managing cash flow is crucial for the financial health of a business. Entrepreneurs need to ensure that they have enough cash to cover expenses, meet financial obligations, and invest in growth opportunities. This involves monitoring and projecting cash inflows and outflows, optimizing payment terms with suppliers and customers, and implementing effective cash flow management strategies.

- **Financial Planning and Forecasting:** Entrepreneurs should create a comprehensive financial plan and forecast to guide their business decisions. This involves developing a budget, projecting revenue and expenses, conducting financial analysis, and setting financial goals. Financial planning helps entrepreneurs track their progress, make informed decisions, and adapt their strategies as needed.

- **Risk Management:** Entrepreneurs need to assess and manage various financial risks associated with their business. This may include risks such as market fluctuations, competition, regulatory changes, credit risk, and operational risks. Implementing risk management strategies, such as diversifying revenue streams, obtaining insurance coverage, and maintaining emergency funds, can help entrepreneurs mitigate financial risks.

- **Financial Reporting and Compliance:** Entrepreneurs must maintain accurate financial records and comply with applicable financial regulations and reporting requirements. This includes keeping track of income and expenses, filing taxes, preparing financial statements, and adhering to accounting standards. Entrepreneurs may need to seek professional assistance from accountants or financial advisors to ensure compliance and accurate financial reporting.

These are some of the key financial considerations and steps that entrepreneurs should keep in mind when starting and operating a business. Being financially savvy and proactive can contribute to the long-term success and sustainability of their entrepreneurial ventures.

Let's try some questions related to business expenses.

1   John earns a monthly salary of $3,500 from his full-time job. He decides to start his own business, which costs him $1,200 per month to run. Calculate John's total monthly income and expenses.

2   Samantha earns a monthly salary of $4,000 from her full-time job. She decides to start her own business, which requires her to pay $500 for equipment and $300 for monthly rent. Calculate Samantha's total monthly income and expenses.

3   Anna earns a monthly salary of $3,000 from her full-time job. She estimates that by starting her own business, she can generate monthly revenue of $5,000 although her business expenses would amount to $4,500. Should Anna quit her full-time job to start this business?

4   John is considering starting a new business. He currently earns a monthly salary of $2,500 from his full-time job. He estimates that his monthly personal expenses amount to $1,800. If he starts the business, he expects his monthly

business expenses to be $1,200. Calculate John's monthly income and savings after deducting personal and business expenses.

5   Sarah is considering starting a new business. She currently earns a monthly salary of $3,000 from her full-time job. Her monthly personal expenses amount to $2,000. If she starts the business, she expects her monthly business expenses to be $1,500. Calculate Sarah's monthly income and savings after deducting personal and business expenses.

6   Emily earns a monthly salary of $2,800 from her full-time job. Her monthly personal expenses amount to $1,500. If she starts the business, she expects her monthly business expenses to be $800. Calculate Emily's monthly income and savings after deducting personal and business expenses.

7   Alex earns a monthly salary of $3,500 from his full-time job. His monthly personal expenses amount to $2,000. If he starts the business, he expects his monthly business expenses to be $1,200. Calculate Alex's monthly income and savings after deducting personal and business expenses.

8   John wants to start a small bakery. He needs to take out a loan of $50,000 to cover the initial setup costs. The bank offers him a loan with an interest rate of 8% per year. If the loan term is 5 years, calculate the total amount John will have to repay, including interest.

9   Sarah wants to start a graphic design business. She needs to take out a loan of $25,000 to purchase necessary equipment. The bank offers her a loan with an interest rate of 6.5% per year. If the loan term is 3 years, calculate the total amount Sarah will have to repay, including interest.

10 Imagine you have decided to become an entrepreneur and start a digital marketing agency. You've invested 20,000 Euros of savings into launching your business, which includes website development, marketing materials, and initial client acquisition efforts. After a year of hard work, your business starts generating a consistent income of 3,000 Euros per month, covering your personal and business expenses.

However, your life takes a significant turn: you get married and soon after, you and your spouse welcome a baby. With the arrival of your child, you now have additional expenses, including medical and baby-related expenses of 300 Euros per month.

A How might your decision to become an entrepreneur impact your personal financial stability, especially considering the initial investment and income fluctuations that often accompany startup ventures?

B With the arrival of a child, what adjustments and financial considerations should you make to ensure your family's financial well-being?

C How can you strike a balance between pursuing your entrepreneurial dream and providing financial security for your family during these challenging circumstances?

Conclusion

- Congratulations on completing the financial literacy course!
- During the course, we explored various areas, such as budgeting, saving, investing, understanding credit and debt, and making informed financial decisions. These topics are vital for your success in navigating the complex world of personal

finance. By gaining knowledge and skills in financial literacy, you have taken a significant step towards securing a better financial future.

- Remember, financial literacy is not a one-time achievement but an ongoing journey. As you move forward, continue to apply the principles and strategies you have learned. Regularly review your budget, track your expenses, and save consistently. Explore different investment options to grow your wealth over time, and make smart choices when it comes to borrowing and managing credit.

- Financial literacy is about being proactive and empowered. It's about understanding the importance of setting financial goals, planning for the future, and being prepared for unexpected expenses. By implementing the knowledge gained from this course, you can build a solid financial foundation that will serve you well throughout your life.

- Always stay curious and continue learning about personal finance. Stay updated on current financial trends, seek advice from trusted sources, and never hesitate to ask questions. Remember, the more you know, the better equipped you will be to make sound financial decisions§.

- As you embark on your journey toward financial independence and security, remember that financial literacy is a lifelong skill. By being mindful of your financial choices, practicing discipline, and staying informed, you have the power to create a bright financial future for yourself.

- Wishing you all the best in your financial endeavors!

- All course content, including text, design, layout, videos and illustrations are original and protected by copyright law. While unauthorized reproduction of this material is strictly prohibited, you are permitted to use this material solely for instructional purposes within your own educational setting.

ANSWERS

Unit 1. What is Financial Literacy?

Section 1.2 Quiz

1 What is debt?
Correct Answer: D

2 What is interest?
Correct Answer: B

3 What is a budget?
Correct Answer: C

4 What is a credit score used for?
Correct Answer: A

5 What is the definition of income?
Correct Answer: D

6 What does saving involve?
Correct Answer: A

7 What is credit?
Correct Answer: A

8 What are expenses?
Correct Answer: C

9 What is an investment?
Correct Answer: D

10 What is identity theft?
Correct Answer: B

11 What is compound interest?
Correct Answer: B

12 What is insurance?
Correct Answer: C

13 What is diversification?
Correct Answer: C

14 What is entrepreneurship?
Correct Answer: D

15 What is gross income?
Correct Answer: A

16 What is net income?
Correct Answer: B

17 What is inflation?
Correct Answer: A

18 Where are shares of publicly traded companies bought and sold?
Correct Answer: B

19 What is financial planning?
Correct Answer: B

20 What is commission?
Correct Answer: C

21 What is a paycheck?
Correct Answer: D

22 What are taxes?
Correct Answer: D

23 What is retirement planning?
Correct Answer: C

24 What is a mortgage?
Correct Answer: A

25 What is a credit card?
Correct Answer: C

26 What is financial literacy?
Correct Answer: A

27 What is estate planning?
Correct Answer: C

28 What is an asset?
Correct Answer: B

29 What is a liability?
Correct Answer: C

30 What is net worth?
Correct Answer: B

31 What is financial risk?
Correct Answer: B

32 What is cash flow?
Correct Answer: B

33 What is liquidity?
Correct Answer: C

34 What is bankruptcy?
Correct Answer: C

35 What is amortization?
Correct Answer: A

36 What is a dividend?
Correct Answer: B

37 What is capital?
Correct Answer: B

38 What is principal?
Correct Answer: B

39 What is a mutual fund?
Correct Answer: A

40 What is a stock?
Correct Answer: A

41 What is a bond?
Correct Answer: A

42 What is a bear market?
Correct Answer: D

43 What is a bull market?
Correct Answer: A

44 What is a budget deficit?
Correct Answer: B

45 What is a budget surplus?
Correct Answer: A

46 What is a will?
Correct Answer: D

47 What is a checking account?
Correct Answer: A

48 What is a savings account?
Correct Answer: A

49 What is a credit report?
Correct Answer: D

50 What is a financial institution?
Correct Answer: C

51 What is a down payment?
Correct Answer: A

52 What is a credit limit?
Correct Answer: C

53 What is a minimum payment?
Correct Answer: B

54 What is a tax deduction?
Correct Answer: A

55 What is a tax credit?
Correct Answer: A

56 What is a prepayment penalty?
Correct Answer: C

57 What is a capital gain?
Correct Answer: A

58 What is a capital loss?
Correct Answer: A

59 What is revenue?
Correct Answer: C

60 What is a loan?
Correct Answer: B

61 What is capital appreciation?
Correct Answer: A

62 What is capital depreciation?
Correct Answer: C

63 What is inventory?
Correct Answer: B

64 What is personal finance?
Correct Answer: D

65 What is sales tax?
Correct Answer: B

66 What is income tax?
Correct Answer: D

67 What is corporate tax?

Correct Answer: B

68 What is taxable income?

Correct Answer: C

69 What is profit?

Correct Answer: B

70 What is a gratuity?

Correct Answer: B

71 What is investment income tax?

Correct Answer: B

72 What is inheritance tax?

Correct Answer: C

73 What is capital gains?

Correct Answer: B

74 Your equity in a home increases if:

Correct Answer: C

75 What is an employee?

Correct Answer: C

76 What is an employer?

Correct Answer: C

77 During a recession it is common to observe:

Correct Answer: B

78 What is an entrepreneur?

Correct Answer: C

79 What is a variable cost?

Correct Answer: B

80 What is cryptocurrency?

Correct Answer: A

81 What is a fixed cost?

Correct Answer: B

82 Correct Answer: B. False

83 Correct Answer: B. False

84 Correct Answer: B. False

85 Correct Answer: B. False

86 Correct Answer: A. True

87 Correct Answer: A. True

88 Correct Answer: B. False

89 Correct Answer: A. True

90 Correct Answer: B. False

Unit 2. Making Informed Purchasing Decisions

Section 2.1 Discounts and Sale Prices

1   $270

2   $102

3   $675

4   $320

5   $105

6   $63

7   $112.50

8   $90

9   Store A: 25% of $80 = $20 off. Store B: $10 off. Therefore, Store A's coupon offers a better deal.

10   Store E: $5 off. Store F: 20% of $30 = $6 off. Therefore, Store F's coupon offers a better deal.

11   Store G: 40% of $50 = $20 off. Store H: $15 off. Therefore, Store G's coupon offers a better deal.

12   Store I: 10% of $70 = $7 off. Store J: $8 off. Therefore, Store J's coupon offers a better deal.

13   Store A = $60

     Store B = $65

     Store C = $72

     Store A saves you the most money with a discount of $20.

14   Store X = $84 × 4 = $336

     Store Y = $100 × 4 = $400

     Store Z = $120 × 2 = $240

     Store Z saves you the most money since you will get two free shampoo bottles.

15 You save the cost of one shampoo, which is $50.

16 $88/$220 × 100 = 40% discount rate.

17 Original price = $110/0.80

Original price = $137.50

18 $20/$100 × 100 = 20%

19 $40 - $5 = $35. You will save $5 with the coupon.

20 0.15 × $200 = $30. You will save $30 with the coupon.

21 You will get back $20 with the coupon.

22 You will get back $16 with the coupon.

23 Store A: $20 × 3 = $6.67 per item. Store B: $35 × 5 = $7 per item.

Store A offers a better deal with a price per item of $6.67.

24 Store A: $12 × 2 = $6 per item. Store B: $26 4 = $6.50 per item.

Store A offers a better deal with a price per item of $6.

Section 2.2 Unit Price and Converting Units of Measure

1   $1.20

2   The price per foot = $0.40

3   The price per inch = $0.02

4   The price per cup is $0.35

5   The price per ounce = $0.05

6   The price per kg = $7

7   The price per liter = $7.20

8   The price per kg is $2.20 (rounded to the nearest cent)

9   The price per gallon is $5.02 (rounded to the nearest cent)

10 The soil costs $1.00 per pound

11 The paint costs $4.43 per quart

Section 2.3 Comparing Offers

1. Both stores have the same unit rate of $0.30 per pen.

2. Both stores have the same unit rate of $0.50 per cookie.

3. FreshFarm: $1.50 per pound. FruitMart: $1.40 per pound.

   FruitMart has a lower unit rate of $1.40 per pound, so it offers a better price per pound for apples compared to FreshFarm.

4. Both stores have the same unit rate of $0.25 per ounce, so they offer the same price per ounce.

5. SportsGear: $15 ÷ 10 = $1.50 per tennis ball. PlayPro: $10 ÷ 6 ≈ $1.67 per tennis ball. SportsGear has a lower unit rate of $1.50 per tennis ball, so it offers a better price per tennis ball compared to PlayPro.

6. Both stores have the same unit rate of $0.01 per page, so they offer the same price per page.

7. CoffeeHouse: $8 ÷ 12 ≈ $0.67 per ounce. BrewCafe: $12 ÷ 16 = $0.75 per ounce

   CoffeeHouse has a lower unit rate of $0.67 per ounce, so it offers a better price per ounce compared to BrewCafe.

8. Both stores have the same unit rate of $2 per hour, so they offer the same price per hour.

Section 2.4 Comparing Options

1. Option 1: Total cost = $19.99

   Option 2: Total cost = $1.29 × 20 = $25.80

   Therefore, the monthly subscription plan (option 1) is more financially sensible for Jenna.

2. Option 1: Monthly book subscription service cost per month = $19.99 + ($1.25 × 3) = $23.74

   Option 2: Total cost = $2.99 × 8 = $23.92

Therefore, the monthly book subscription service is slightly more financially sensible for Emily.

3   The cost of renting a movie from the local store is $2.49, while the cost of the streaming service is $15 per month.

If Alex watches 6 movies per month, the cost of renting would be 6 x $2.49 = $14.94, while the cost of the streaming service would be $15. Therefore, renting movies from the local store is slightly cheaper.

4   The cost of the gym membership per month is $30, while the cost of a daily pass is $2.25 each time. If Amy goes to the gym three times a week, the cost of daily passes would be 3 x 4 weeks x $2.25 = $27 per month. Therefore, the daily passes are more cost effective.

5   To calculate the cost per year, divide the total cost by the expected lifespan. For the repaired laptop: $150/3 years = $50/year. For the new laptop: $800/5 years = $160/year. Therefore, the repaired laptop has a lower cost per year.

6   Total cost of the used bike = $200 + $50 = $250. By choosing the used bike, Mark can save $100 compared to buying a new bike ($350 - $250).

7   Annual savings = ($50 - $10) × 12 months = $480

8   Cost for the hair dryer = $40 for two years.

Cost for hair salon visits = $1 × 2 visits/month × 24 months = $48. The hair dryer is the more cost-effective option.

9   Cost per month for monthly membership = $50. Cost per month for annual membership = $500/12 months = $41.67. Since the annual membership has a lower cost per month, it is the more cost-effective option.

10 Cost of cafe coffee in a month: $3.65 × 20 = $73. Cost of coffee beans in a month to brew 20 cups of coffee: $10 × 4 = $40.

Savings per month by brewing her own coffee: $73 - $40 = $33

11 Cost of cooking at home for 7 days = $375

Cost of eating at a restaurant: ($20 × 1.05) × 3 meals × 7 days = $441

Cost of ordering food delivery: ($30 × 1.02) × 3 meals × 7 days = $642.60

Based on the calculations, cooking at home is the most cost-effective option per week.

Let's Explore

12 Option 1: Cost without warranty: $1,000

Option 2: Cost with warranty: $1,150

Expected Repair/Accidental Damage Cost = Probability of Repair x cost of Repair

0.60 × $1,000 = $600

In this scenario, the expected repair and accidental damage cost is higher than the cost of the warranty. Given that Emily will rely heavily on the laptop as well as the relatively high likelihood of needing repairs or encountering accidental damage, it is probably a good idea for Emily to purchase the warranty.

13 Option 1: Cost without warranty = $800

Option 2: Cost with warranty = $975

Since Sarah plans on replacing the phone with a new one next year, she could forgo purchasing the warranty and apply the $175 towards her new phone next year. However, she should still consider the risks of repair costs if she purchases the phone without a warranty.

14 Option 1: Cost without warranty = 3 × $800 = $2,400

Option 2: Cost with warranty = $2,400 + $200 = $2,600

Expected Repair Cost: 0.10 × $2,400 = $240

Even though they estimate only a 10% chance of needing repairs, Tom and Lisa might find value in the warranty due to the cumulative potential repairs on multiple appliances and the convenience of a bundled coverage.

Section 2.5 Square Footage Price and Property Comparison

1   Casablanca: $300,000/1,500 = $200/sq. ft

    Willows Creek: $360,000/1,800 = $200/sq. ft

    The price per square foot is the same for both properties.

2   Property 1: $200/sq ft

    Property 2: 167.86/sq ft

    Property 3: $210/sq. ft

    Property 2 offers the best value based on lowest price per square foot.

3   10,000/10.764 = 929.03 sq meters (rounded to two decimal places)

    929.03 × $250 = $232,257.50

    The cost of purchasing the land is approximately $232,257.50.

4   Apartment A: $200 × 10.764 = $2,152.80 per square foot.

    Apartment B has a lower cost per square foot ($20/sq ft)

5   150 sq meters × 10.764 = 1,614.6 sq ft

    1,614.6 sq ft × 14 AED/sq ft = AED 22,604.40

6   (a) Service charges: 14 EUR × 450 = 6,300 EUR

    (b) Commission: 0.02 × 500,000 EUR = 10,000 EUR

7   (a) 250 × AED 10 = AED 2,500

    (b) AED 27,650 × 0.05 = AED 1,382.50

Section 2.6 Currency Exchanges

1   202.50 AED

2   400 AED × (1 GBP/4.25 AED) = 94.12 GBP (rounded to two decimal places). Sara received 94.12 GBP.

3   250 GBP/1,250 AED. 1 AED = 0.20 GBP

4   1,500 AED x (1 GBP/4.75 AED) = 315.79 GBP (rounded to two decimal places)

5   150 GBP × 4.60 AED/GBP = 690 AED

6   20,000 NGN × (1 USD/400 NGN) = 50 USD

7   1,500 USD/500,000 NGN = 0.003

    1 NGN = 0.003 USD

8   $1,200 × 410 NGN/USD = 492,000 NGN

9   1,000,000 NGN × (1 USD/380 NGN) = 2,631.58 USD (rounded to two decimal places)

10 USD 500 × 440 NGN/USD = 220,000 NGN

11 1,500 CAD × (0.57 JOD/CAD) = 855 JOD

12 4,250 JOD/10,000 CAD. 1 CAD = 0.425 JOD

13 80 JOD × (1 CAD/0.43 JOD) = 186.05 CAD (rounded to two decimal places)

14 2,000 CAD × (0.50 JOD/CAD) = 1,000 JOD

15 500 CAD × 0.56 JOD/CAD = 280 JOD

16 500 GBP/2,500 AED. 1 AED = 0.20 GBP

17 $800 × 16.50 ZAR/USD = 13,200 ZAR

18 2,500 CAD × (0.55 JOD/CAD) = 1,375 JOD

19 600 GBP × 5.10 AED/GBP = 3,060 AED

20 1,000 EUR × (1.50 AUD/EUR) = 1,500 AUD

21 1,750 EUR /2,500 AUD. I AUD = 0.70 EUR

22 600 EUR × 1.20 AUD/EUR = 720 AUD

23 3,200 EUR /5,000 AUD. I AUD = 0.64 EUR

24 800 EUR × 1.40 AUD/EUR = 1,120 AUD

25 2,000 ARS × (0.06 BRL/ARS) = 120 BRL

26 1,500 COP × (0.003 PEN/COP) = 4.50 PEN

27 100,000 CLP × (0.09 ARS/CLP) = 9,000 ARS

28 500 BRL × (8.50 UYU/BRL) = 4,250 UYU

29 1,000 PEN × (0.60 BOB/PEN) = 600 BOB

30 100,000 JPY × (1 USD/110 JPY) = 909.09 USD (rounded to two decimal places)

31 50,000 JPY × (1 USD/112 JPY) = 446.43 USD (rounded to two decimal places)

32 111,000 JPY/1,000 USD. 111 JPY = 1 USD

33 200,000 JPY × (1 AUD/85 JPY) = 2,352.94 AUD (rounded to two decimal places)

34 50,000 INR × (1 GBP/100 INR) = 500 GBP

35 5,000 INR × (1 USD/75 INR) = 66.67 USD (rounded to two decimal places)

36 75,000 INR/1,000 USD. I USD = 75 INR

37 10,000 INR × (1 CAD/55 INR) = 181.82 CAD (rounded to two decimal places)

38 Cost in USD: 0.05 ETH × $2,500/ETH = $125

39 Cost in USD: 0.1 BTC × $40,000/BTC = $4,000

40 Cost in USD: 800 EUR × 1.15USD/EUR = 920 USD

Section 2.7 Renting v. Buying

1   For purchasing: Total cost = $25,000

For renting: Total cost = $400 × 12 months/year × 5 years.

Total cost = $24,000

In this case, renting costs less.

2   For purchasing: Total cost = $60

For renting: Total cost = $1.20 × 52 weeks. Total cost = $62.40.

In this case, purchasing the textbook costs less than renting.

3   For purchasing: Total cost = $79.99

For renting: Total cost = $13.50 × 6 occasions = $81

In this case, purchasing the dress of $79.99 is more financially sensible.

4   For purchasing: Total cost = $800

For renting: $40 × 12 months/year × 2 years = $960

In this case, purchasing is more cost-effective since the total cost of purchasing is $800, which is lower than the total cost of renting at $960.

5   For purchasing: Total cost = $200

For renting: Total cost = $15 × 10 days = $150

In this case, renting is more financially sensible since the total cost of renting is $150, which is lower than the total cost of purchasing at $200.

Let's Explore

6   Compare the cost of leasing to the total cost of buying:

Lease cost: $14,400 for a 48 month term.

Purchase cost: $27,108.12 ($564.75/month for 48 months)

$5,000 (down payment) + $20,000 (loan principal) + $2,108.12 (interest)

Buying a Car

Pros:

- Ownership: You build equity and eventually own the car.

- Long-term savings: Usually, buying a car will lead to savings compared to the cost of continued leasing.

- No mileage limits: You can drive as much as you want without worrying about mileage penalties that may apply to leased cars.

- Customization: You can modify and personalize the car to your liking.

Cons:

- Higher initial costs: Down payments can be high or financially difficult to obtain.

- Depreciation: The car's value depreciates over time, affecting resale value.

- Maintenance costs: You are responsible for all maintenance and repairs once the warranty expires.

- Risk of obsolescence: The car's technology and features might become outdated.

Leasing a Car

Pros:

- Lower initial costs: Typically requires a smaller down payment or fee upfront compared to purchasing.

- Easy Transitions: You can drive a new car with the latest features every few years.

- Limited repair costs: The car is usually under warranty for the lease duration.

Cons:

- No ownership: You don't build equity or own the car at the end of the lease (unless it is a rent-to-own type of contract).
- Mileage limits: Exceeding mileage limits results in additional charges.
- Wear and tear penalties: You'll pay for excessive wear and tear on the car.
- Higher long-term costs: Continually leasing can be more expensive in the long run.
- Early termination fees: Exiting the lease early can be costly.

Ultimately, the decision depends on your preferences, financial situation and how long you plan to keep the car. If you value ownership and plan to keep the car for a long time, then buying may be better. If you prefer lower monthly payments and like having a new car every few years, then leasing could be more suitable.

7   Compare the cost of leasing to the total cost of buying property.

Cost of leasing: $18,000 per year ($1,500/month)

Cost of buying: $472,486.82 ($1,145.80/month for 30 years)

$60,000 (down payment) + $240,000 (principal) + $172,486.82 (interest)

Leasing

Pros:

- Lower initial costs: Leasing requires a smaller upfront payment compared to purchasing.
- Flexibility: Leasing allows you to move easily at the end of a lease term.
- Less responsibility: Major maintenance and repair costs are often the landlord's responsibility.

Cons:

- No equity: You don't build equity or ownership in the property (unless it is a lease-to-own arrangement).
- Rent increases: Landlords can increase rent after the lease term.
- Limited customization: You may have restrictions on how you can personalize the property.
- Other restrictions: The landlord may not allow you to have pets.

Buying

Pros:

- Equity building: Mortgage payments contribute towards building ownership and equity.
- Long-term investment: Real estate can appreciate, potentially leading to financial gains.
- Stability: Your monthly mortgage payments remain relatively stable over time.
- Personalization: You have more freedom and flexibility to customize and modify your property.

Cons:

- Higher initial costs: Purchasing requires a larger down payment and closing costs.
- Long-term commitment: You are tied to the property for the duration of the mortgage (unless you decide to sell the property).
- Maintenance and associated costs: You are responsible for all maintenance and repairs, as well as applicable property tax.
- Market risk: Property values can fluctuate, affecting potential resale value.

- Higher monthly payments: Monthly mortgage payments can end up being higher than rent.

- Cost of borrowing: Cost of borrowing, especially with higher interest rates can be financially draining.

Ultimately, the decision between leasing and purchasing depends on your financial situation, long-term goals and personal preferences. If you value ownership, building equity and stability, then purchasing may be the better choice. However, if you prefer flexibility and lower initial costs, leasing may be the better choice.

Unit 3. Budgeting

Section 3.1 Multiple Purchases and Budgeting

1   Yes. Total cost of items = $45 + $30 + $20 = $95

2   No. Total cost of three items = $800 + $102 + $27 = $929

3   No. Total cost of items after discount: $41.50

4   No. Total cost of items after discount: $217.50

5   $100 + $1 + $15 - $50 = $66

6   0.20 × $400 = $80

7   Yes, since you will still have $150 after paying rent and monthly expenses.

8   No. $250 + $30 = $280. If you purchase the phone you will only have $20 left.

9   Amount allocated to savings = $150

Amount allocated to spending = $200

Amount allocated to donating = $150

10 Amount allocated to accommodation = $400

Amount allocated to transportation = $250

Amount allocated to activities = $350

11 Amount allocated to groceries = $300

Amount allocated to dining out = $180

Amount allocated to entertainment = $120

12 Amount allocated to clothes = $480

Amount allocated to shoes = $200

Amount allocated to accessories = $120

13 Amount allocated to savings = $120

Amount allocated to spending = $160

Amount allocated to charity = $120

14 Amount allocated to clothes = $240

Amount allocated to electronics = $360

Amount allocated to books = $600

15 Amount saved for the concert ticket = $200

Amount spent on the phone = $150

Amount allocated to going out = $150

16 Amount allocated to donations = $120

17 John should allocate $150 for books, $200 for meals, $100 for entertainment, and $50 for other expenses.

18 Emily should allocate $245 for meals, $140 for entertainment, and $157.50 each for books and other expenses.

19 $350

20 $780

21 $60

22 $4,800

23 $600

24 No, Dana cannot afford all the items on the list because the total cost of the items is: $2.50 + $3.00 + $2.20 + $8.50 + $4.00 = $20.20

Section 3.2 50/30/20 Rule

1 John should allocate $1,500 for needs, $900 for wants, and $600 for savings and debt repayment.

2 Mary should allocate $2,500 for needs, $1,500 for wants, and $1,000 for savings and debt repayment.

3 Sara should allocate $1,250 for needs, $750 for wants, and $500 for savings and debt repayment.

4   Wants (30% of income) = \$1,350. Therefore, if he spends \$1750 on vacation he will exceed the 30% "Wants" allocation under the 50/30/20 rule.

5   Needs = 0.5 × \$6,000 = \$3,000. Yes, Nafisa can spend \$2,500 on the braces she needs, while following to the 50/30/20 rule.

6   Needs: Rent, groceries

Wants: Dining out, Netflix subscription, new iphone 13

Savings/Debt Repayment: Retirement fund

7   Needs: Health insurance, utility bills

Wants: Movie tickets, gym membership

Savings/Debt Repayment: Emergency fund, vacation savings

Let's Explore

8   a) The unexpected car repair bill of \$800 could disrupt your original plans to purchase the gadget and go on vacation. Depending on what is still unused under your "savings" portion of \$600, you may be able to use that for your car repair bill, along with \$200 from your "wants" category. Since there would only be \$700 left for "wants," you would likely have to delay purchasing the \$300 gadget, although you would still have sufficient funds to go on vacation for \$600. (Alternatively, you could decide to forgo the vacation and purchase the gadget instead).

b) Factors to consider:

- Urgency of the car repair: Is it a safety concern or can it wait?

- Importance of the vacation and gadget: Can you delay these purchases without significant consequences?

- Emotional satisfaction vs. financial security: Balancing the immediate gratification of wants against the importance of being financially prepared for emergencies.

c) Having an emergency fund in place would give you the peace of mind to confidently handle unexpected expenses. If you had set aside an emergency fund, you could use it to cover the car repair bill without sacrificing your original plans. This helps you maintain a sense of financial stability while ensuring that you can still pursue your goals without compromising your financial well-being.

Unit 4. Shared Costs

Section 4.1 Dividing the Bill and Tip

1   $34.50

2   $28.80

3   $22.13 (rounded to the nearest cent)

4   $38.33 (rounded to the nearest cent)

5   You pay $60 and the remaining three people each pay $20.

6   You will pay $56 while your three friends will each pay $36.

7   $60

8   The friend who can only pay half of their portion will pay $16/2 = $8.

Therefore, you and the other three friends will each pay $16 + $2 = $18.

9   Person A's percentage = 20%

Person B's percentage = 16.67%

Person C's percentage = 23.33%

Person D's percentage = 13.33%

Person E's percentage = 26.67%

Section 4.2. Dividing the Rent

1   You will pay $1,680, while the remaining three roommates will each pay $373.33 (rounded to the nearest cent)

2   Your contribution = $40,000/$150,000 = 4/15

Friend A's ratio = $50,000/ $150,000 = 1/3

Friend B's ratio = $60,000/ $150,000 = 2/5

Calculate each person's contribution based on their income ratio.

Your contribution = (4/15) × $3,500 = $933.33 (rounded to the nearest cent)

Friend A's contribution = (1/3) × $3,500 = $1,166.67 (rounded to the nearest cent)

Friend B's contribution = (2/5) × $3,500 = $1,400

3   You will pay = $900. The remaining rent: $2,400 = $1,500

Malika pays: $1,500 × 0.75 = $1,125

Shinaya pays: $1,500 × 0.25 = $375

4   The friend who stayed only for three days will pay a total of $$337.50. The three people who remain for the entire six days will pay $787.50 each.

5   Rent: You and Ibrahim will each pay = $360

Amjad and Mike will each pay $240

Electricity: You will pay: $75 × 0.32 = $24

Ibrahim, Amjad and Mike will each pay: $17

Total paid by each: You ($384), Ibrahim ($377), Amjad ($257), Mike ($257)

6   Karima pays $960, while you and Amari each pay $720.

7   Daily rate: $2,050/7 = $292.86 (rounded to two decimal places)

Cost per person first three days: $292.86/3 x 3 days = $292.86

Cost per person last four days: $292.86/2 x 4 days = $585.72

Joe should pay approximately: $292.86

You and Mary should each pay approximately: $292.86 + $585.72 = $878.58

8   Your room: (600 ÷ 2,000) × $1,800 = $540

Roommate A's room: (500 ÷ 2,000) × $1,800 = $450

Roommate B's room: (400 ÷ 2,000) × $1,800 = $360

Roommate C's room: (500 ÷ 2,000) × $1,800 = $450

9   Rushabh and Arman will each pay $1,250 per month during the first two months. Isht will not pay any rent since he will not join the lease and move in during the first two months.

10 $0.47 \times \$150 = \$70.50$

$0.19 \times \$98 = \$18.62$

Rubin will pay a total of $89.12

11 Julie will only pay $30.

You, Mariam and Fatima will each pay: $60 + $10 = $70.

12 Your room: $80 ÷ 9 = $8.89 (rounded to the nearest cent)

Roommate A's room: $80 ÷ 9 × 2 = $17.78 (rounded to the nearest cent)

Roommate B's room: $80 ÷ 9 × 3 = $26.67 (rounded to the nearest cent)

Roommate C's room: $80 ÷ 9 × 2 = $17.78 (rounded to the nearest cent)

Roommate D's room: $80 ÷ 9 = $8.89 (rounded to the nearest cent)

13 Kumar will pay $30, while you and Ajesh will each pay $45.

14 Your room: $90 ÷ 8 × 2 = $22.50

Roommate A's room: $90 ÷ 8 × 1 = $11.25

Roommate B's room: $90 ÷ 8 × 3 = $33.75

Roommate C's room: $90 ÷ 8 × 2 = $22.50

15 You, Brigitte and Isabelle will each pay ($260 x 8) + $346.67 (rounded to nearest cent) = $2,426.67. Florence will pay $260 × 8 = $2,080.

16. Your room: (400 ÷ 1,200) × $80 = $26.67 (rounded to the nearest cent)

    Roommate A's room: (300 ÷ 1,200) × $80 = $20

    Roommate B's room: (200 ÷ 1,200) × $80 = $13.33 (rounded to the nearest cent)

    Roommate C's room: (300 ÷ 1,200) × $80 = $20

17. You will pay $480 in rent. Your roommates will each pay $240 in rent.

    You will pay $70 in utilities. Your two roommates will each pay $35 in utilities.

    You will pay a total of $480 + $70 = $550

    Both roommates will each pay a total of $240 + $35 = $275.

18. Madonna, Kylie and Kim will each pay approximately $28.13 (rounded to the nearest cent). Chloe will pay approximately $5.63 (rounded to the nearest cent).

Let's Explore

19. a) If one of your roommates doesn't pay their share of the rent or moves out unexpectedly, it can create financial challenges such as:

    • You and your other roommate will need to cover the missing portion of the rent, which can strain your budget and disrupt your financial plans (including the 50/30/20 budget rule).

    • If you have signed a lease indicating that you are "jointly and severally liable" you could be held legally liable for the full rent amount and not just your individual portion.

    • Unpaid rent can result in late fees imposed by the landlord, which can add to the financial burden.

    • Financial disagreements can strain your relationship with roommates.

(b) The security deposit is typically held by the landlord to cover any damages beyond normal "wear and tear." If a roommate causes significant damage, it could lead to deductions from the security deposit, affecting the amount, if any, returned at the end of the lease.

- Depending on the lease agreement, roommates might be jointly held responsible for damages. This can lead to disagreements about who is financially accountable for the repair costs.

- Disagreements over damage-related costs can strain relationships among roommates, leading to conflict and a less harmonious living situation.

(c) To ensure a smooth co-living experience with roommates and address potential issues, consider the following steps:

- Establish open lines of <u>communication</u> from the beginning. Discuss expectations for rent payment, bill sharing and responsibilities.

- Build <u>an emergency fund</u> to cover unexpected expenses or roommate situations, such as someone leaving suddenly.

- Consider <u>tenant insurance</u> to protect your belongings and provide liability coverage in case of accidents or damages.

- Discuss and establish how the <u>security deposit</u> will be handled and returned, especially in cases of damage or roommate changes.

- Consider a process for resolving conflicts, whether it's about finances, living arrangements or personal issues.

Unit 5. Taxes

Section 5.1 Sales Tax

1   Total cost = $25 + $1.75 = $26.75

2   Total cost = $800 + $72 = $872

3   Total cost = $65 + $3.90 = $68.90

4   Total cost = $15 + $1.20 = $16.20

5   Total cost = $120 + $12 = $132

6   Total cost = $45.00 + $3.60 = $48.60

7 $85

8 $30

9 $50

10 $9

11 $6.18 (rounded to the nearest cent)

Section 5.2 Tax and Gratuity

1   Total cost = $45 + $3.15 + $7.22 = $55.37

2   Total cost = $35 + $2.80 + $7.00 = $44.80

3   Total cost = $75 + $5.25 + $13.50 = $93.75

4   Total cost = $8 + $0.72 + $1.74 = $10.46

5   Total cost =$50 + $4 + $7.50 = $61.50

6   Total amount: $120 + $7.20 + $26.40 = $153.60

7   (a) Tax 8.93 + tip $16.75 = $25.68

   (b) Amount before tax and tip: $111.65

Section 5.3 Income Tax

1 Total Tax Liability = $1,000 + $1,500 + $1,000 = $3,500.

2 Total Tax Liability = $1,000 + $750 = $1,750.

3 Total Tax Liability = $400 + $1,200 + $750 = $2,350.

4 Total Tax Liability = $400 + $200 = $600.

5 Total Tax Liability = $3,000 + $7,500 + $3,000 = $13,500.

6 Total Tax Liability = $2,250.

7 Total Tax Liability = $3,000 + $7,500 + $3,500 = $14,000.

8 Total Tax Liability = $2,000.

9 Total Tax Liability = $1,000 + $3,000 + $1,250 = $5,250.

10 (a) $14,750

(b) $295

11 Total Tax Liability = $1,500 + $2,250 = $3,750.

12 Total Tax Liability = $1,000.

13 Total Tax Liability = $2,500 + $4,500 + $1,000 = $8,000.

14 (a) $42,500

(b) $2,125

Section 5.4 Investment Tax

a. Capital Gains Tax

1 $500 × 0.20 = $100.

2 $2,000 × 0.15 = $300.

3 $50,000 × 0.25 = $12,500.

4 $2,500 × 0.10 = $250.

5 $50,000 × 0.30 = $15,000.

b. Dividend Tax

1 $$1,500 \times 0.15 = \$225.$

2 $$2,000 \times 0.20 = \$400.$

3 $$500 \times 0.10 = \$50.$

4 $$5,000 \times 0.25 = \$1,250.$

5 $$10,000 \times 0.30 = \$3,000.$

c. Interest Income Tax

1 $$500 \times 0.10 = \$50.$

2 $$200 \times 0.20 = \$40.$

3 $$2,500 \times 0.25 = \$625.$

4 $$5,000 \times 0.30 = \$1,500.$

d. Rental Income Tax

1 $$14,400 \times 0.20 = \$2,880.$

2 $$30,000 \times 0.15 = \$4,500.$

3 (a) $10,400

   (b) $12,480

4 (a) $21,000

   (b) $27,000

Section 5.5 Property Tax

1 Annual property tax = $250,000 × 0.012 = $3,000

2 Taxable value = $400,000 × (1 - 0.20) = $320,000

   Annual property tax = $320,000 × 0.008 = $2,560

3 Taxable value = $180,000 - $2,000 = $178,000

   Annual property tax = $178,000 × 0.025 = $4,450

4   Property tax = $300,000 × 0.015 = $4,500

School tax = $300,000 × 0.007 = $2,100

Total annual property tax = $4,500 + $2,100 = $6,600

5   Tax up to $150,000 = $150,000 × 0.01 = $1,500

Tax above $150,000 = ($220,000 - $150,000) × 0.015 = $1,050

Total annual property tax = $1,500 + $1,050 = $2,550

Section 5.6 Inheritance Tax

1   $500,000 × 0.10 = $50,000.

2   $2,000,000 × 0.20 = $400,000.

3   $1,500,000 × 0.15 = $225,000.

4   $800,000 × 0.25 = $200,000.

5   $3,500,000 × 0.30 = $1,050,000.

6   $75,000 + $12,500 = $87,500.

7   $112,500 + $150,000 = $262,500.

8   $2,000,000 × 0.05 = $100,000.

9   $60,000 + $6,000 = $66,000.

10 $400,000 + $150,000 = $550,000.

Section 5.7 Corporate Tax

1   $500,000 × 0.25 = $125,000.

2   $1,200,000 × 0.30 = $360,000.

3   $750,000 × 0.20 = $150,000.

4   $2,500,000 × 0.35 = $875,000.

5   $1,800,000 × 0.28 = $504,000.

6   $400,000 × 0.22 = $88,000.

7 $\$1,000,000 \times 0.32 = \$320,000.$

8 $\$3,600,000 \times 0.29 = \$1,044,000.$

9 $\$550,000 \times 0.27 = \$148,500.$

10 $\$900,000 \times 0.24 = \$216,000.$

11 Tax deductions normally lower the amount of an individual's taxable income.

$(\$500,000 - \$50,000) \times 0.25 = \$112,500$

12 Tax credits are normally subtracted from the taxes owed.

$\$800,000 \times 0.30 = \$240,000.$

$\$240,000 - \$100,000 = \$140,000$

13 $\$1,050,000 \times 0.20 = \$210,000.$

14 $AED3,000,000 \times 0.12 = AED\ 360,000$

$AED\ 360,000 - AED\ 39,500 = AED\ 320,500$

Unit 6. Managing Bank Accounts and Savings

1   New balance = $650

2   New balance = $430

3   Mary will have a positive balance of $600.

4   John will have a positive balance of $600.

5   Sarah will have a positive balance of $150.

6   David will have a positive balance of $200.

7   Emily will have a positive balance of $150.

8   Mark will have a zero balance.

9   Emma will have a positive balance of $100.

10 Michael will have a positive balance of $150.

11 Olivia will have a positive balance of $100.

12 Daniel will have a negative balance of $650.

13 Both options result in the same total savings of $240.

14 Saving $2 every day for one year = $730

Saving $14 every week for one year = $728

Saving $2 a day would result in a higher total savings of $730.

15 Saving $5 per day for one year = $1,825

Saving $200 every month for 6 months = $1,200

Saving $5 per day for one year would result in higher savings of $1,825.

16 Saving $1.50 every day for 140 days = $210

Saving $10.00 every week for 140 days = $200

Saving $1.50 a day would result in a higher total savings of $210.

17 Saving $20 every week for 26 weeks = $520

Saving $80 every month for 6 months = $480

Saving $20 every week would result in a higher total savings of $520.

18 Saving $3 every day for 240 days = $720

Saving $21 every week for 8 months = $672

Saving $3 a day would result in a higher total savings of $720.

19 Saving $2 per day for 5 years = $3,650

Saving $14 per week for 5 years = $3,640

Saving $60 per month for 5 years = $3,600

Saving $2 per day would result in the highest total savings of $3,650.

20 Saving $5 per day for 3 years = $5,475

Saving $35 per week for 3 years = $5,460

Saving $150 per month for 3 years = $5,400

Saving $5 per day would result in the highest total savings of $5,475.

21 Saving $3 per day for 8 years = $8,760

Saving $21 per week for 8 years = $8,736

Saving $90 per month for 8 years = $8,640

Saving $3 per day would result in the highest total savings of $8,760.

22 Saving $1 per day for 2 years = $730

Saving $7 per week for 2 years = $728

Saving $30 per month for 2 years = $720

Saving $1 per day for 2 years would result in the highest total savings of $730.

23 Saving $2 per day for 4 years = $2,920

Saving $14 per week for 4 years = $2,912

Saving $60 per month for 4 years = $2,880

Saving $2 per day would result in the highest total savings of $2,920.

24 Saving $3 per day for 3 years = $3,285

Saving $21 per week for 3 years = $3,276

Saving $90 per month for 3 years = $3,240

Saving $3 per day for 3 years would result in the highest total savings of $3,285.

25 Saving $2 per day for 3 years = $2,190

Saving $10 per week for 3 years = $1,560

Saving $40 per month for 3 years = $1,440

Saving $2 per day would result in the highest total savings of $2,190.

26 Saving $3 per day for 5 years = $5,475

Saving $20 per week for 5 years = $5,200

Saving $80 per month for 5 years = $4,800

Saving $3 per day would result in the highest total savings of $5,475.

27 Saving $1 per day for 4 years = $1,460

Saving $7 per week for 4 years = $1,456

Saving $30 per month for 4 years = $1,440

Saving $1 per day would result in the highest total savings of $1,460.

28 Saving $1.50 per day for 10 years = $5,475

Saving $5 per week for 10 years = $2,600

Saving $40 per month for 10 years = $4,800

Saving $1.50 per day would result in the highest total savings of $5,475.

29 Saving $3 per day for 10 years = $10,950

Saving $15 per week for 10 years = $7,800

Saving $80 per month for 10 years = $9,600

Saving $3 per day would result in the highest total savings of $10,950.

30 Saving $2 per day for 10 years = $7,300

Saving $10 per week for 10 years = $5,200

Saving $50 per month for 10 years = $6,000

Saving $2 per day would result in the highest total savings of $7,300.

31 Saving $3 per day for 10 years = $10,950

Saving $20 per week for 10 years = $10,400

Saving $100 per month for 10 years = $12,000

Saving $100 per month would result in the highest total savings of $12,000.

32 Saving $2.50 per day for 10 years = $9,125

Saving $15 per week for 10 years = $7,800

Saving $60 per month for 10 years = $7,200

Saving $2.50 per day would result in the highest total savings of $9,125.

33 Saving $5 per day for 10 years = $18,250

Saving $30 per week for 10 years = $15,600

Saving $200 per month for 10 years = $24,000

Saving $200 per month would result in the highest total savings of $24,000.

Unit 7. Interest

Section 7.1 Simple Interest

1 $2,500 × 0.08 × 3 = $600

2 $1,000 × 0.05 × 2 = $100

3 $3,000 × 0.10 × 1.5 = $450

4 $5,000 × 0.06 × 4 = $1,200

5 $800 × 0.075 × 2 = $120

6 $2,500 × 0.04 × 3 = $300

7 $1,200 × 0.09 × 2.5 = $270

8 $4,000 × 0.055 × 5 = $1,100

9 $2,500 × 0.06 × 1.5 = $225

10 $3,000 × 0.035 × 4 = $420

11 $4,500 × 0.0725 × 3 = $978.75

12 $6,000 × 0.0475 × 2.5 = $712.50

13 $1,000 × 0.065 × 1 = $65

14 $5,000 × 0.0225 × 3.5 = $393.75

15 $1,500 × 0.0875 ×2 = $262.50

16 $2,000 × 0.0325 × 4.5 = $292.50

17 $2,200 × 0.055 × 3 = $363

18 $4,500 × 0.04 × 2.5 = $450

19 $3,800 × 0.0625 × 1.5 = $356.25

20 $5,500 × 0.045 × 5 = $1,237.50

21 Interest: $500 × 0.5 × 3 = $75

Total savings after 3 years: $500 + ($25 × 3) = $575

22 Interest: $200 × 0.4 × 2= $16

Total savings after 2 years: $200 + $16 = $216

23 Interest: $1,500 × 0.025 × 4 = $150

Total savings after 4 years: $1,500 + $150 = $1,650

Section 7.2 Compound Interest

(Use the compound interest formula to solve the questions in this section)

1   Approximately $788.13

2   Approximately $492.36

3   Approximately $1,264.93

4   Approximately $563.58

5   Approximately $941.28

6   Approximately $1,637.66

7   Approximately $4,830.60

8   Approximately $1,351.33

9   Approximately $2,039.38

10 Approximately $1,399.30

11 Approximately $11,897.60

12 Approximately $13,172.50

13 Approximately $16,192.75

14 Approximately $18,692.73

15 Approximately $3,049.22

16 Approximately $3,204.43

17 Approximately $3,438.65

18 Approximately $30,783.67

19 Approximately $6,245.91

20 Approximately $5,368.46

Section 7.3 Interest on Savings (Simple and Compound)

1   Principal + (Principal × Interest Rate x Time)

Total savings = \$500 + (\$500 × 0.5 × 3) = \$575

2   Future Value = $\$1{,}000 \times (1 + 0.03/12)^{(12*5)}$

Future Value = $\$1{,}000 \times (1.0025)^{(60)}$

Future Value = Approximately \$1,161.62

3   Principal + Simple Interest: \$200 + (\$200 × 0.04 × 2) = \$216

Total savings = \$216

4   Balance: \$1,500 + (\$37.50 × 4) = \$1,650

5   Total savings: \$300 + \$18 = \$318

6   Total savings: $\$2{,}000 \times (1+0.045/2)^{(2*3)}$

$\$2{,}000 \times (1.0225)^{6}$

Total savings: Approximately \$2,285.65

7   Total savings: \$400 + (\$8 × 5) = \$440

8   AED $3{,}500 \times (1+0.035/12)^{(12*2)}$

= AED $3{,}500 \times (1+ 0.00291667)^{24}$

Total savings = Approximately AED 3,753.40

9   Total savings: \$600 + (\$600 x 0.015 × 4) = \$636

10 Total savings: GBP $4{,}000 \times (1 + 0.02/4)^{(4*3)}$

GBP $4{,}000 \times (1+0.005)^{12}$

Total savings = Approximately GBP 4,246.71

11 Total savings: 500 EUR + (20 EUR × 5) = 600 EUR

12 Total savings: JOD $1{,}200 \times (1+ 0.035/4)^{(4*2)}$

JOD $1{,}200 \times (1+ 0.00875)^{8}$

Total savings = Approximately JOD 1,286.62

Unit 8. Investing

Section 8.1 Return on Investments

1	50%	16	20%
2	25%	17	25%
3	25%	18	30%
4	33.33%	19	30%
5	20%	20	20%
6	20%	21	-10%
7	30%	22	- 15%
8	20%	23	-25%
9	30%	24	-40%
10	20%	25	-40%
11	20%	26	-20%
12	25%	27	-20%
13	25%	28	-20%
14	20%	29	-20%
15	20%	30	-40%

Section 8.2 Compounding Investments

1 Approximately $6,230.91

2 Approximately $12,314.39

3 Approximately $2,827.46

4 Approximately $1,565.68

5 Approximately $8,689.88

6 (a) $1,200,000

(b) $1,210,000

(c) $1,215,506.25

(d) $1,219,391.08

7 FV of Maryam's investment = $5,000 $(1+0.00583333)^{24}$

$5,000 (1.149805926)

$5,749.03

FV of Josh's investment = $5,000 × $(1+0.07)^{\wedge 2}$

FV = $5,724.50

8 (a) Year 1: $1,000 + $60 = $1,060

(b) Year 2: $1,060 + $63.60 = $1,123.60

Let's Explore

9 (a) (i) The rule of 72: number of years × interest rate = 72

Years to double = 72/4 = 18

(i) Years to double = 72/10 = 7.2

(b) (i) Interest rate: 72/5 = 14.4%

(ii) Interest rate: 72/10 = 7.2%

(iii) 72/15 = 4.8%

Section 8.3 Cryptocurrency

1 Total Cost = $50,000

Transaction Fee for Buying = $50,000 × 2% = $1,000

Total Selling Price = $75,000

Transaction Fee for Selling = $75,000 × 2% = $1,500

Profit or Loss = $75,000 - $50,000 - $1,000 - $1,500 = $22,500

Therefore, Bob's total profit after considering the transaction fees is $22,500.

2   Approximately $5,832

3   Total Mining Rewards = 365,000 coins

Percentage = (365,000 coins/10,000,000 coins) x 100

Percentage = 3.65%

Therefore, the mining rewards in the first year represent 3.65% of the total supply.

4   Percentage Increase = ((Final Investment Value - Initial Investment)/Initial Investment) × 100

Percentage Increase = (($1.20 - $0.50)/$0.50) × 100

Therefore, Sarah's investment increased by 140%.

5   $0.40 – $0.20 = $0.20 per unit.

50 units × $0.20 = $10

Therefore, Jackson profited $10 from selling 50% of his cryptocurrency holdings.

6   Percentage Loss = ((Initial Investment Value – Final Investment Value)/Initial Investment Value) × 100

Percentage Loss = (($1.00 - $0.80) / $1.00) × 100

Therefore, Emma incurred a loss of 20% on her investment.

7   Final Investment Value = Initial Investment + Return on Investment

Final Investment Value = $5,000 + $750

Therefore, the final investment value after one year is $5,750.

8   $3.75/unit × 43 units = $161.25

Therefore, Lily received a total amount of $161.25 from selling 43 units of her cryptocurrency holdings.

9   $3,000 × (1 + 0.10)^6

$5,314.68

10 $3,000 × (1 +0.10/12)^6

$3,153.16

1   (a) Daily interest rate: 0.17/365 = 0.00046575 or 0.046675%

(b) $10,000 + (0.00046575 × $10,000) = $10,004.66

2   Daily interest rate: 0.16/365 = 0.00043836

$1,200 × 0.00043836 = $0.5260274 (rounded to $0.53)

$0.53 × 30 days = $15.90

Interest charged for billing cycle: Approximately $15.90

3   $3,500/$200 = 17.5 months.

4   $6,000 x 0.03 = $180.

5   $4,000/36 = $111.11 (rounded to two decimal places). Daniel should make a monthly payment of approximately $111.11.

6   $2,800/12 = $233.33 (rounded to two decimal places). Sophia should make a monthly payment of approximately $233.33.

7   Interest = Principal × Interest Rate × Time

Interest = $200 × 0.18 × (1/12) = $3.00

8   Interest = Remaining balance × Interest Rate × Time

$400 × 0.20 × (1/12) = $400 × 0.20/12 = $400 × 0.0167 = $6.67

9   $1,600 + $631 - $419 = $1,812

Minimum payment: $1,812 × 0.08 = $144.96

10 $3,150 × 0.195 = $614.25

Monthly interest: 614.25/12 = $51.19

Total balance: $3,150 + $51.19 = $$3,201.19

Minimum monthly payment: 0.02 × $3,201.19 = $64.02

11 Convert the annual interest rate to a monthly rate: 0.18/12 = 0.015 per month.

Interest = Outstanding Balance × Monthly Interest = $500 × 0.015 = $7.50.

12 Interest: 0.432/12 × ($305.62 - $125 +$290)

=0.036 × $470.62 = $16.94

13 Convert the annual interest rate to a monthly rate: 0.18/12 = 0.015 per month.

Interest = Outstanding Balance x Monthly Interest Rate x Number of Months = $800 × 0.015 × 2 = $24.

14 (a) Interest = Outstanding Balance × Monthly Interest Rate × Number of Months

= $2,500 x 0.0167 × 2 = Approximately $83.50.

(b) Principal + Interest + Penalty

Penalty: $2,583.50 × 0.01 = $25.84

Total: $2,500 + $83.50 + $25.84 = Approximately $2,609.34

15 Minimum payment: $2,500 × 0.03 = $75

16 Convert the annual interest rate to a monthly rate: 0.24/12 = 0.02 per month.

Interest = Outstanding Balance x Monthly Interest Rate x Number of Months = $3,000 × 0.02 × 3 = $180.

17 Convert the annual interest rate to a daily rate: 0.16/365 = 0.00043836

Interest = Outstanding Balance × Daily Interest Rate × Number of Days

$1,500 × 0.00043836 × 45 days = $29.59

18 Closing balance. $$2,650 + $277 - $30 = $2,897

Minimum monthly payment: $2,897 × 0.21 = $608.37

19 Closing balance: $3,560 - $300 = $3,260

Minimum monthly payment: $3,260 × 0.02 = $65.20

20 0.065/365 = Approximately 0.018%

21 $3,100 × 0.18/365 × 40 = $61.15

22 0.14/365 = 0.00038356

Interest = Outstanding Balance × Daily Interest Rate

= $2,000 × 0.00038356 = Approximately $0.77

23 0.21/12 = 0.0175 per month.

Interest = Outstanding Balance × Monthly Interest Rate × Number of Months = $3,000 × 0.0175 × 1 = $52.50

Amount owed after one month: $3,000 + $52.50 = $3,052.50

24 0.18/365 = 0.00049315

Interest = Outstanding Balance × Daily Interest Rate × Number of Days = $1,200 × 0.00049315 × 50 days = $29.59

Amount owed after 50 days: $1,200 + $29.59 = $1,229.59

25 (a) June minimum payment: 0.09 × $622 = $55.98.

(b) Interest: 0.42/12 × ($622-$55.98) = 0.035 × $566.02 = $19.81

(c) New balance: $622 - $55.98 + $19.81 = $585.83

(d) July minimum payment: 0.09 × $585.83 = $52.72

26 (Answers may vary slightly due to rounding of numbers).

Interest = 0.44/12 × ($340 - $110 + $1,215) = 0.0367 × $1,445 = $53.03

New Balance: $340 - $110 + $1,215 + $53.03 = $1,498.03

	Previous Balance	Payments	Purchases	Interest	New Balance
Month 1	$340	$110	$1,215	$53.03	$1,498.03

(Answers may vary slightly due to rounding of numbers).

27 (Answers may vary slightly due to rounding of numbers).

Interest = 0.44/12 × ($1,498.03 - $85 + $450) = 0.0367 × $1,863.03 = $68.37

New Balance: $1,498.03 - $85 + $450 + $68.37 = $1,931.40

	Previous Balance	Payments	Purchases	Interest	New Balance
Month 1	$340	$110	$1,215	$53.03	$1,498.03
Month 2	$1,498.03	$85	$450	$68.37	$1,931.40

Section 9.2 Loans

a) Simple Interest Loans

1 (a) the total amount to be repaid is $5,450

(b) the monthly payment is $227.08

2 Interest = $10,000 × 0.06 x 3.5 = $2,100

Total Amount = $10,000 + $2,100 = $12,100

Monthly Payment = $12,100/(3.5 × 12) = $288.10

(a) the total interest paid is $2,100

(b) the monthly payment is $288.10

3 Interest = $8,500 x 0.0375 × 4 = $1,275

Total Amount = $8,500 + $1,275 = $9,775

Monthly Payment = $9,775/(4 × 12) = $203.65

(a) the total amount to be repaid is $9,775

(b) the monthly payment is $203.65

4 Interest = $15,000 × 0.0525 × 2.5 = $1,968.75

Total Amount = Principal + Interest

(a) Total Amount = 15,000 + $1,968.75 = $16,968.75

(b) Monthly Payment = $16,968.75 /(2.5 × 12) = $565.63

5 Interest = $12,500 × 0.04 × 6 = $3,000

(a) Total Amount = $12,500 + $3,000 = $15,500

(b) Monthly Payment = $15,500/(6 × 12) = $215.28

6 Interest = $20,000 × 0.065 × 1.5 = $1,950

(a) Total Amount = $20,000 + $1,950 = $21,950

(b) Monthly Payment = $21,950/(1.5 × 12) = $1,219.44

7 Interest = $6,000 × 0.0225 × 3 = $405

(a) Total Amount = $6,000 + $405 = $6,405

(b) Monthly Payment = $6,405/(3 × 12) = $177.92

8 Interest = $9,500 × 0.0475 × 2 = $902.50

(a) Total Amount = $9,500 + $902.50 = $10,402.50

(b) Monthly Payment = $10,402.50/(2 × 12) = $433.44

9 Interest = $25,000 × 0.07 × 5 = $8,750

(a) Total Amount = $25,000 + $8,750 = $33,750

(b) Monthly Payment = $33,750/(5 × 12) = $562.50

10 Interest = $7,500 × 0.035 × 4.5 = $1,181.25

(a) Total Amount = $7,500 + $1,181.25 = $8,681.25

(b) Monthly Payment = $8,681.25/(4.5 × 12) = $160.76

11 Interest = $18,000 × 0.05 × 3 = $2,700

(a) Total Amount = $18,000 + $2,700 = $20,700

(b) Monthly Payment = $20,700/(3 × 12) = $575

12 Interest = $10,500 × 0.0425 × 2.75 = $1,227.19

(a) Total Amount = $10,500 + $1,227.19 = $11,727.19

(b) Monthly Payment = $11,727.19/(2.75 × 12) = $355.37

13 Interest = $14,000 × 0.039 × 4.25 = $2,320.50

(a) Total Amount = $14,000 + $2,320.50 = $16,320.50

(b) Monthly Payment = $16,320.50/(4.25 × 12) = $320

14 Interest = $8,000 × 0.045 × 3.5 = $1,260

(a) Total Amount = $8,000 + $1,260 = $9,260

(b) Monthly Payment = $9,260/(3.5 x 12) = $220.48

15 Interest = $11,200 × 0.0575 × 2.25 = $1,449

(a) Total Amount = $11,200 + $1,449 = $12,649

(b) Monthly Payment = $12,649/(2.25 x 12) = $468.48

b) Compound Interest Loans

1 $10,000 x $(1 + 0.06/12)^{42}$ = $12,330.33

(a) Total interest paid = $2,330.33

(b) Monthly payment = $293.58

2 $8,500 x $(1 + 0.0375/12)^{48}$ = $9,873.28

(a) Total interest paid = $1,373.28

(b) Monthly payment = $205.69

3 $15,000 x $(1 + 0.0525/12)^{30}$ = $17,098.90

(a) Total interest paid = $2,098.90

(b) Monthly Payment =$569.96

4 $12,500 x $(1 + 0.04/12)^{72}$ = $15,884.27

(a) Total interest paid = $3,384.27

(b) Monthly Payment = $220.61

5 $20,000 x $(1+ 0.065/12)^{18}$ = $22,042.43

(a) Total interest paid = $2,042.43

(b) Monthly Payment = $1,224.58

6    $6,000 x (1 + 0.0225/12)^{36} = $6,418.58

(a) Total interest paid = $418.58

(b) Monthly Payment = $178.29

7    $9,500 x (1+ 0.0475/12)^{24} = $10,444.80

(a) Total interest paid = $944.80

(b) Monthly Payment = $435.20

8    $25,000 x (1 + 0.07/12)^{60} = $35,440.63

(a) Total interest paid = $10,440.63

(b) Monthly Payment = $590.68

9    $7,500 x (1 + 0.035/12)^{54} = $8,777.34

(a) Total interest paid = $1,277.34

(b) Monthly Payment = $162.54

10   $18,000 x (1 + 0.05/12)^{36} = $20,906.50

(a) Total interest paid = $2,906.50

(b) Monthly Payment = $580.74

11   $10,500 x (1 + 0.0425/12)^{33} = $11,799.34

(a) Total interest paid = $1,299.34

(b) Monthly Payment = $357.56

Let's Explore

12   (a) Total cost of borrowing on simple interest loan:

$10,000 × 0.05 x 5 = $2,500

Total cost of borrowing = $10,000 + $2,500 = $12,500

(b) Total cost of borrowing on compound interest loan:

$10,000 × (1+0.05/12)$^{(12*5)}$

Total cost: $12,833.59

(c) In this scenario, the total cost of borrowing in option (b) is higher due to the compounding interest being charged on the borrowed amount.

Other factors to consider when choosing between loan options:

- Compare interest rates to determine overall cost.

- Loans with higher compounding frequencies (ie. monthly) tend to accumulate more interest.

- Calculate the total cost of borrowing or total amount you will have to repay for each loan option.

- Consider the term length. Longer terms might result in lower monthly payments but higher total interest paid.

- Calculate the monthly payment for each loan option to ensure it fits your budget.

- Check if there are any prepayment penalties or flexibility to pay off the loan early.

- Consider your current financial status and stability before committing to any loan.

c) Amortized Loan Formula

(Apply the amortization formula to calculate monthly payments. See example in Question section).

1   $466.08

2   $472.00

3   $449.56

4   $442.88

5   $522.44

6   $432.36

7   $465.95

8   $478.88

9   $429.09

10 $736.73

11 $431.04

12 $426.35

13 $425.20

14 $384.92

15 $389.12

16 $342.52

17 $315.79

18 $291.39

19 $351.00

20 (a) $366.28

(b) $366.28 x 36 payments = $13,186.08

Total interest paid: $13,186.08 - $12,500 = $686.08

21 (a) $204.02

(b) Cost of borrowing: $204.02 × 48 payments = $9,792.96

22 (a) $363.41

(b) $363.41 × 72 payments = $26,165.52

Total interest paid: $26,164.52 - $22,500 = $3665.52

(i) Amortization Schedule

To fill out each row of an amortization table/schedule, you need to follow these steps:

1   In the first row, insert "0" in the Payment Number column and the initial amount loaned in the Remaining Principal/Balance" column.

2   Calculate the fixed monthly payment using the amortization formula and insert the monthly payment amount in the Amount of Payment column in the 2nd row.

3   Calculate the Interest Paid by multiplying the periodic interest by the remaining principal (from the previous row).

4   Calculate the Principal Paid by subtracting the Interest Paid from the Payment Amount.

5   Subtract the Principal from the Remaining Principal (in the previous row).

6   Continue the sequence until you reach the last row and the Remaining Principal is zero. (Since amounts may be rounded, the final amount may be +/- by a few cents).

Monthly Payment Amount

Monthly Payment = $P \times (r(1+r)^n) / ((1+r)^n - 1)$

Monthly Payment = $100,000 \times (0.00149167(1+0.00149167)^{12})/ ((1+0.00149167)^{12} - 1)$

Monthly Payment = $100,000 \times ((0.00149167) \times (1.018047628))/0.18047628$

Monthly Payment = $8,414.35. (rounded to two decimal places)

Interest Payment

Interest = Remaining Principal x Periodic Interest Rate

First interest payment: $100,000 \times 0.0179/12 = \$149.17$

Second interest payment: $91,734 \times 0.0179/12 = \$136.84$

Principal Paid

Payment Amount - Interest Paid

First Principal Paid amount: $8414.35 - $149.17 = $8265.18

Second Principal Paid amount: $8414.35 - 136.84 = $8,277.51

Subtract the Principal Paid from Remaining Principal

For Remaining Principal in row 2: $100,000 - $8265.18 = $91,734.82

For Remaining Principal in row 3: $91,734.82 - 8277.71 = $83,457.31

Payment Number	Payment Amount	Interest Paid	Principal Paid	Remaining Principal
0				100,000
1	8,414.35	149.17	8265.18	91,734.82
2	8,414.35	136.84	8277.51	83,457.31
3	8,414.35	124.49	8289.86	75,167.45
4	8,414.35	112.13	8302.22	66,865.23
5	8,414.35	99.74	8314.61	58,550.62
6	8,414.35	87.34	8327.01	50,223.61
7	8414.35	74.92	8339.43	41,884.18
8	8414.35	62.48	8351.87	33,532.31
9	8414.35	50.02	8364.33	25,167.98
10	8414.35	37.54	8376.81	16,791.17
11	8414.35	25.05	8389.30	8,401.87
12	8414.35	12.53	8401.82	0.05

Unit 10. Mortgages

1   $1,667.50

2   (a) $1,667.50 × 300 payments = $500,250

   (b) $500,250 - $300,000 = $200,250

3   20%

4   $320,000

5   $50,000

6   20%

7   360

8   $7,381.00

9   $400,000 × 0.035 = $14,000

10 ($150,000 × 0.0525)/12 = $656.25

11 $2,588.91

12 Monthly = $1,157.79

   Total payments for first year: $1,157.79 × 12 = $13,893.48

13 $2,639.82

14 $3,761.39

15 ($350,000 × 0.07)/12 = $,2041.67

16 Monthly: $2,147.29

   $2,147.29 × 360 payments = $773,024.40

   Total interest: $773,024.40 - $400,000 = $373,024.40

17 Mortgage amount = $175,000 - $26,250 = $148,750

   Monthly payment: $1,148.08

   Total cost: $1,148.08 × 300 payments = $344,424

18 Monthly property tax: $2,356/12 = $196.33

Monthly mortgage + property tax: $965.23 + $196.33 = $1,161.56

19 $1,900,000 × 0.07 = $133,000

Unit 11. Purchasing Power

Section 11.1 Exponential Decay

1   $664.83

2   $f(x) = \$1,000 \times (1 - 0.06)^9$

$f(x) = \$1,000 \times 0.5729948022$

$f(x) \approx \$572.99$

3   $f(x) = \$500 \times (1 - 0.015)^8$

$f(x) = \$500 \times 0.8861145015$

$f(x) \approx \$443.06$

4   $f(x) = \$1,000(1 - 0.05)^{10}$

$f(x) = \$1,000 \times 0.5987369392$

$f(x) \approx \$598.74$

5   $f(x) = \$10,000(1 - 0.045)^{15}$

$f(x) = \$10,000(0.5012456005)^{15}$

$f(x) = \$5,012.46$

6   (a) $f(x) = \$100 \times (1 - 0.05)^1$

$f(x) = \$95$. Therefore, you can purchase 9 bottles of shampoo.

(b) $f(x) = \$100 \times (1 - 0.05)^2$

$f(x) = \$90.25$. Therefore, you can purchase 9 bottles of shampoo.

(c) $f(x) = \$100 \times (1 - 0.05)^3$

$f(x) = \$85.74$. Therefore, you can buy 8 bottles of shampoo.

(d) $f(x) = \$100 \times (1 - 0.05)^8$

$f(x) = \$66.34$. Therefore, you can buy 6 bottles of shampoo.

Section 11.2 Exponential Growth

1   $f(x) = \$5{,}000 \,(1 + 0.07)^{15}$

   $f(x) = \$13{,}795.16$

2   $f(x) = 200{,}000 \times (1 + 0.05)^{10}$

   $f(x) = 325{,}778.93$ rupees

3   $f(x) = 1{,}500 \times (1 + 0.02)^{16}$

   $f(x) = 2{,}059.18$ Euros

4   $f(x) = \$1{,}000 \times (1 + 0.05)^{10}$

   $f(x) = \$1{,}000 \times (1.628894627)$

   $f(x) = \$1{,}628.89$

5   (a) $f(x) = \$100 \times (1 + 0.10)^{1}$

      $f(x) = \$110$. You can purchase 11 bottles of shampoo.

   (b) $f(x) = \$100 \times (1 + 0.10)^{2}$

      $f(x) = \$121$. You can purchase 12 bottles of shampoo.

   (c) $f(x) = \$100 \times (1 + 0.10)^{3}$

      $f(x) = \$133.10$. You can purchase 13 bottles of shampoo.

   (d) $f(x) = \$100 \times (1 + 0.10)^{8}$

      $f(x) = \$214.36$. You can purchase 21 bottles of shampoo.

Unit 12. Capital Appreciation and Capital Depreciation

Section 12.1 Capital Appreciation

1   ($15/$50) × 100% = 30%.

2   $50,000/$200,000) × 100% = 25%.

3   ($5,000/$10,000) × 100% = 50%.

4   ($1,300/$2,500) × 100% = 52%.

5   ($10/$20) × 100% = 50%.

6   ($2,500/$5,000) × 100% = 50%.

7   ($15,000/$30,000) × 100% = 50%.

8   ($1,500/$1,000) × 100% = 150%.

9   ($30,000/$50,000) × 100% = 60%.

10 ($15/$10) × 100% = 150%.

Section 12.2 Capital Depreciation

1   $1,600 per year

2   $25,000/10 = $2,500 per year
    The annual straight-line depreciation for the car is $2,500.

3   $1,500/3 = $500 per year
    The annual straight-line depreciation for the computer is $500.

4   $450,000/40 = $11,250 per year
    The annual straight-line depreciation for the building is $11,250.

5   $100,000/5 = $20,000 per year
    The annual straight-line depreciation for the machinery is $20,000.

6   $75,000/8 = $9,375 per year

The annual straight-line depreciation for the equipment is $9,375.

7   Percentage depreciation. ($450,000 - $340,000)/$450,000 x 100 = 24.44%

8   (a) Annual depreciation expense: ($26,700 - $2,500)/5 = $4,840

(b) Capital depreciation percentage: ($26,700 - $2,500)/$26,700 x 100 = 90.64%

(c) Annual rate of depreciation: 90.64%/5 = 18.13%

or: $4,840/$26,700 x 100 = 18.13%

9   ($1,500 - $200)/4 = $325

Book value after 3 years: $1,500 – ($325 x 3) = $525

10 ($458 - $80)/5 = $75.60

Book value after 2 years: $458 – ($75.60 x 2) = $306.80

11 (a) ($80,000 - $5,000)/10 = $7,500

Book value end of year 1 using straight-line: $72,500

Book value end of year 2 using straight-line: $65,000

(b) Year 1 Depreciation: $80,000 × 0.20 + $16,000

Book value end of year 1 using declining balance: $80,000 - $16,000 = $64,000

Year 2 Depreciation: $64,000 × 0.20 = $12,800

Book value end of year 2 using declining balance: $64,000 - $12,800 = $51,200

12 Step 1: Sum of the years' digits for the useful life of the truck

= 6+5+4+3+2+1 = 21 Or 6 × (6 + 1)/2 = 21

Step 2: Calculate the fraction of the sum of the years' digits for each year

Depreciation = (Years remaining/Sum of the years' digits) × (Initial value – Salvage value)

Year 1 Depreciation = (6/21) × ($50,000 - $0) = $14,285.71 (rounded to nearest cent)

Year 2 Depreciation = (5/21) × ($50,000 - $0) = $11,904.76 (rounded to the nearest cent)

Year 3 Depreciation = (4/21) × ($50,000 - $0) = $9,523.81 (rounded to the nearest cent)

Unit 13 Insurance

1   Premium: ($20,000 × 0.05) = $1,000. (The deductible is not included in the premium; it is an amount that is paid out of pocket before the insurance coverage applies).

2   Premium: $300,000 × 0.003 = $900.

3   Multiply the premium rate by the number of people covered by the policy: Monthly Premium = $200 × 4 = $800.

4   Premium: ($100,000/1,000) × $10 = $100 × $10 = $1,000.

5   Premium: $1,500,000 × 0.02 = $30,000.

6   Total Premium: ($20 × 3) × 2 = $120.

7   Annual Premium: $0.10 × 10,000 = $1,000.

8   Monthly Premium: ($50 × 2) + $70 = $100 + $70 = $170.

9   Monthly Premium: ($200,000/100) × $1.50 = $2,000 × $1.50 = $3,000.

10   Annual Premium: $8,000 × 0.08 = $640.

11   Annual Premium: $50,000 × 0.002 = $100.

12   Annual Premium: ($500,000 / 1,000) × $20 = $500 × $20 = $10,000.

13   Annual Premium: $2,000,000 × 0.015 = $30,000.

14   Total Premium: ($10 × 5) × 7 = $350.

15   Annual Premium: $0.25 × 20,000 = $5,000.

16   Monthly Premium: ($40 × 3) + ($60 × 2) = $120 + $120 = $240.

17   Monthly Premium: ($300,000/100) × $2 = $3,000 × $2 = $6,000.

18   Annual Premium: $5,000 × 0.10 = $500.

19   Annual Premium: $400,000 × 0.0025 = $1,000.

20   Annual Premium = ($250,000/1,000) × $15 = $250 × $15 = $3,750.

Unit 14. Retirement Planning

Section 14.1 Saving Early and The Power of Compounding

1    $\$300 \times ((1 + .005)^{420} - 1)/0.005$

     $\$300 \times (8.123551494 - 1)/0.005$

     $\$300 \times 7.123551494/0.005$

     $\$300 \times 1424.71$

     FV = $\$427,413.09$

2    $\$300 \times ((1+0.005)^{180} - 1)/0.005$

     $\$300 \times (2.454093562 - 1)/0.005$

     FV = $\$87,245.61$

3    $FV = AED\ 100 \times ((1+0.00416667)^{564} - 1)/0.00416667$

     FV = AED 226,428.31

4    $FV = AED\ 100 \times ((1 + 0.00416667)^{240} - 1)/0.00416667$

     FV = AED 41,103.39

Section 14.2 Estimate Retirement Needs - the "70 - 80% rule"

1    $\$60,000 \times 0.75 = \$45,000$ per year

2   GBP 80,000 × 0.70 = GBP 56,000 per year

3   100,000 Euros × 0.76 = 76,000 Euros

4   500,000 Rupees × 0.80 = 400,000 Rupees

Unit 15. Business

Section 15.2 Financial Documents and Business Expenses

Cost of Goods Sold (COGS):

Use the following formula to calculate the COGS.

Beginning inventory + purchases of inventory – ending inventory = COGS

1   To calculate COGS, we need to subtract the ending inventory from the sum of beginning inventory and purchases:

COGS = Beginning Inventory + Purchases - Ending Inventory

COGS = $10,000 + $5,000 - $8,000

COGS = $7,000

Therefore, the Cost of Goods Sold (COGS) for the month amounts to $7,000.

2   COGS = Beginning Inventory + Purchases - Ending Inventory

COGS = $40,000 + $20,000 - $15,000 COGS = $45,000

3   COGS = Beginning Raw Material Inventory + Raw Material Purchases - Ending Raw Material Inventory

COGS = $30,000 + $50,000 - $25,000 COGS = $55,000

4   COGS = Beginning Inventory + Purchases - Ending Inventory

COGS = $15,000 + $8,000 - $6,000 COGS = $17,000

5   COGS = Beginning Inventory + Purchases - Ending Inventory

COGS = $60,000 + $25,000 - $40,000 COGS = $45,000

6   COGS = Beginning Inventory + Purchases - Ending Inventory

COGS = $10,000 + $5,000 - $8,000 COGS = $7,000

7   COGS = Beginning Inventory + Purchases - Ending Inventory

COGS = $10,000 + $20,000 - $8,000 COGS = $22,000

Therefore, the cost of goods sold for the bookstore is $22,000.

8   COGS = Beginning Inventory + Purchases - Ending Inventory
COGS = \$50,000 + \$30,000 - \$40,000 COGS = \$40,000

Therefore, the cost of goods sold for the grocery store is \$40,000.

Gross Profit Margin

1   Gross Profit Margin = ((\$800,000 - \$600,000) / \$800,000) × 100

Gross Profit Margin = (\$200,000 / \$800,000) × 100

Gross Profit Margin = 0.25 × 100

Gross Profit Margin = 25%

2   Gross Profit Margin = ((\$1,200,000 - \$800,000)/\$1,200,000) × 100

Gross Profit Margin = (\$400,000/\$1,200,000) × 100

Gross Profit Margin = 0.3333 × 100

Gross Profit Margin = 33.33%

3   Gross Profit Margin = ((\$400,000 - \$200,000)/\$400,000) × 100

Gross Profit Margin = (\$200,000/\$400,000) × 100

Gross Profit Margin = 0.5 100

Gross Profit Margin = 50%

4   Gross Profit Margin = ((\$2,000,000 - \$1,200,000)/\$2,000,000) × 100

Gross Profit Margin = (\$800,000/\$2,000,000) × 100

Gross Profit Margin = 0.4 × 100 Gross Profit Margin = 40%

5   Gross Profit Margin = ((\$300,000 - \$100,000)/\$300,000) × 100

Gross Profit Margin = (\$200,000/\$300,000) × 100

Gross Profit Margin = 0.6667 × 100

Gross Profit Margin = 66.67%

6 Gross Profit Margin = (($1,000,000 - $700,000)/$1,000,000) × 100

Gross Profit Margin = ($300,000/$1,000,000) × 100

Gross Profit Margin = 0.3 × 100

Gross Profit Margin = 30%

Net Income

1 Net Income = Total Revenues - Cost of Goods Sold - Operating Expenses

Net Income = $50,000 - $25,000 - $12,000

Net Income = $13,000

2 Net Income = Total Sales - Cost of Services - Operating Expenses Net Income = $100,000 - $35,000 - $20,000

Net Income = $45,000

3 Net Income = Total Revenue - Cost of Goods Manufactured - Operating Expenses + Non-Operating Income

Net Income = $500,000 - $250,000 - $150,000 + $25,000

Net Income = $125,000

4 Net Income = Total Sales - Cost of Food and Beverages Sold - Operating Expenses - Non-Operating Expense

Net Income = $200,000 - $80,000 - $60,000 - $5,000

Net Income = $55,000

5 Net Income = Total Revenue - Cost of Software Development - Operating Expenses + Interest Income

Net Income = $1,000,000 - $500,000 - $300,000 + $10,000

Net Income = $210,000

6 Net Income = Revenue - Cost of Goods Sold - Expenses

Net Income = $500,000 - $300,000 - $150,000

Net Income = $50,000

7   Net Income = Revenue - Cost of Goods Sold - Expenses

Net Income = $800,000 - $600,000 - $200,000

Net Income = $0

8   Net Income = Revenue - Cost of Goods Sold - Expenses

Net Income = $1,200,000 - $0 - $800,000

Net Income = $400,000

9   Net Income = Revenue - Cost of Goods Sold - Expenses

Net Income = $400,000 - $150,000 - $200,000

Net Income = $50,000

10 Net Income = Revenue - Cost of Goods Sold - Expenses

Net Income = $2,000,000 - $1,200,000 - $820,000

Net Income = -$20,000, indicating a net loss of ($20,000).

11 Net Income = Revenue - Cost of Goods Sold - Expenses

Net Income = $300,000 - $100,000 - $250,000

Net Income = -$50,000, indicating a net loss of ($50,000).

12 Net Income = Revenue - Cost of Goods Sold - Expenses

Net Income = $1,000,000 - $700,000 - $400,000

Net Income = -$100,000, indicating a net loss of ($100,000).

Break-Even Point

1   Break-Even Point = Fixed Costs/(Sales Price per Unit - Variable Cost per Unit)

Break-Even Point = $50,000/($10 - $6)

Break-Even Point = $50,000/$4

Break-Even Point = 12,500 units

2   Break-Even Point = Fixed Costs/(Sales Price per Unit - Variable Cost per Unit)

Break-Even Point = $100,000/($50 - $30)

Break-Even Point = $100,000/$20

Break-Even Point = 5,000 units

3   Break-Even Point = Fixed Costs/(Sales Price per Unit - Variable Cost per Unit)

Break-Even Point = $200,000/($100 - $70)

Break-Even Point = $200,000/$30

Break-Even Point = 6,666.67 units (approximately 6,667 units)

4   Break-Even Point = Fixed Costs/(Sales Price per Unit - Variable Cost per Unit)

Break-Even Point = $80,000/($20 - $12)

Break-Even Point = $80,000/$8

Break-Even Point = 10,000 units

5   Break-Even Point = Fixed Costs/(Sales Price per Unit - Variable Cost per Unit)

Break-Even Point = $30,000/($100 - $20)

Break-Even Point = $30,000/$80

Break-Even Point = 375 units

6   Break-Even Point = Fixed Costs / (Sales Price per Unit - Variable Cost per Unit)

Break-Even Point = $150,000/($200 - $50)

Break-Even Point = $150,000/$150

Break-Even Point = 1,000 units

7   Break-Even Point = Fixed Costs/(Sales Price per Unit - Variable Cost per Unit)

Break-Even Point = $50,000/($500 - $200)

Break-Even Point = $50,000/$300

Break-Even Point = 166.67 units (approximately 167 units)

Return on Investment

1   Return on Investment = ((Amount Generated - Cost of Investment)/Cost of Investment) × 100

(($12,500 - $10,000)/$10,000) × 100

($2,500/$10,000) × 100

0.25 × 100

Return on Investment = 25%

2   Return on Investment = ((Amount Generated - Cost of Investment)/Cost of Investment) × 100

(($100,000 - $50,000)/$50,000) × 100

($50,000 / $50,000) × 100

Return on Investment: 1 × 100

Return on Investment = 100%.

3   Return on Investment = ((Amount Generated - Cost of Investment)/Cost of Investment) × 100

(($6,500 - $5,000)/$5,000) × 100

($1,500/$5,000) × 100

Return on Investment: 0.3 × 100

Return on Investment = 30%.

4   Return on Investment = ((Amount Generated - Cost of Investment)/Cost of Investment) × 100

(($150,000 - $100,000)/$100,000) × 100

($50,000/$100,000) × 100

Return on Investment: 0.5 × 100

Return on Investment = 50%

5   Return on Investment = ((Amount Generated - Cost of Investment)/Cost of Investment) × 100

(($30,000 - $20,000)/$20,000) × 100

($10,000/$20,000) × 100

Return on Investment: 0.5 × 100

Return on Investment = 50%

Differentiating Fixed and Variable Costs

1   Fixed costs are expenses that remain constant regardless of the level of production, while variable costs change with the level of production.

Fixed Costs: The fixed costs in this case are the expenses that do not change with the level of production, such as rent, property tax and salaries. Fixed Costs = Rent + Property Tax + Salaries

Fixed Costs: $2,000 + $600 +$5,000 = $7,600

Variable Costs: The variable costs in this case are the expenses that change with the level of production, such as raw materials.

Variable Costs = $3,500

Calculating Monthly Payroll Expenses

1   Total Payroll Expenses = Employee A's Salary + Employee B's Salary + Employee C's Salary + Employee D's Salary + Accountant's Salary

Total Payroll Expenses: $3,500 + $4,200 + $2,800 + $3,900 + $5,500 = $19,900

Calculate Total Assets, Total Liabilities, and Shareholders' Equity

1   Total Assets = Current Assets + Non-Current Assets = $50,000 + $100,000 = $150,000

Total Liabilities = Current Liabilities + Long-Term Liabilities = $30,000 + $50,000 = $80,000

Shareholders' Equity = Total Assets - Total Liabilities = $150,000 - $80,000 = $70,000

Therefore, the total assets are $150,000, total liabilities are $80,000, and shareholders' equity is $70,000.

Section 15.3. Entrepreneurship and Starting a New Business

1   Total Monthly Income = Salary from full-time job = $3,500

Total Monthly Expenses = Business expenses = $1,200

John's total monthly income after deducting business expenses is $3,500 - $1,200 = $2,300.

2   Total Monthly Income = Salary from full-time job = $4,000

Total Monthly Expenses = Equipment cost + Rent = $500 + $300 = $800

Samantha's total monthly income after deducting business expenses is $4,000 - $800 = $3,200.

3   Total Monthly Income from Full-Time Job = $3,000

Total Monthly Income from Business = $5,000

Total Monthly Expenses for Business = $4,500

Anna's total monthly income from the business after deducting expenses is $5,000 - $4,500 = $500. Since $500 is less than her current monthly salary of $3,000, it is more profitable for Anna to continue with her full-time job.

4   Total Monthly Income = Salary from full-time job = $2,500

Total Monthly Personal Expenses = $1,800

Total Monthly Business Expenses = $1,200

John's monthly income after deducting personal expenses is $2,500 - $1,800 = $700.

John's monthly income after deducting personal and business expenses is $700 - $1,200 = -$500.

Since John's monthly income after deducting personal and business expenses is negative, he would not have any savings.

5   Total Monthly Income = Salary from full-time job = $3,000

Total Monthly Personal Expenses = $2,000

Total Monthly Business Expenses = $1,500

Sarah's monthly income after deducting personal expenses is $3,000 - $2,000 = $1,000.

Sarah's monthly income after deducting personal and business expenses is $3,000 - $2,000 - $1,500 = -$500.

Since Sarah's monthly income after deducting personal and business expenses is negative, she would not have any savings.

6 Total Monthly Income = Salary from full-time job = $2,800

Total Monthly Personal Expenses = $1,500

Total Monthly Business Expenses = $800

Emily's monthly income after deducting personal expenses is $2,800 - $1,500 = $1,300.

Emily's monthly income after deducting personal and business expenses is $2,800 - $1,500 - $800 = $500.

Since Emily's monthly income after deducting personal and business expenses is positive, she would have savings of $500.

7 Total Monthly Income = Salary from full-time job = $3,500

Total Monthly Personal Expenses = $2,000

Total Monthly Business Expenses = $1,200

Alex's monthly income after deducting personal expenses is $3,500 - $2,000 = $1,500.

Alex's monthly income after deducting personal and business expenses is $3,500 - $2,000 - $1,200 = $300.

Since Alex's monthly income after deducting personal and business expenses is positive, he would have savings of $300.

8 Interest = Loan Amount x Interest Rate x Loan Term

Interest = $50,000 x 0.08 x 5 = $20,000

Total Amount to Repay = Loan Amount + Interest

Total Amount to Repay = $50,000 + $20,000 = $70,000

John will have to repay a total of $70,000, including interest.

9 Interest = Loan Amount x Interest Rate x Loan Term

Interest = $25,000 x 0.065 x 3 = $4,875

Total Amount to Repay = Loan Amount + Interest Total Amount to Repay = $25,000 + $4,875 = $29,875

Sarah will have to repay a total of $29,875, including interest.

Let's Explore

10 (a) The decision to become an entrepreneur involves both risks and potential rewards. The initial investment of 20,000 Euros impacted your savings, and the income fluctuations during the startup phase can create uncertainty. It's important to be prepared for periods of lower income and have a financial cushion to cover personal and business expenses during these times.

(b) Adjustments and financial considerations:

- Maintain a substantial emergency fund to cover unexpected expenses and business challenges.

- Review your insurance coverage, including health and life insurance, to ensure that you and your family are adequately protected.

- Consider the income and cost scenario if your spouse works (full-time or part-time) and you pay for childcare expenses.

(c) Balancing entrepreneurship an family security:

- Consider planning your family expansion alongside your business growth, if possible, to mitigate financial shocks.

- Explore opportunities to diversify income streams or build passive income sources to ensure greater financial stability.

- Regularly communicate with your spouse about financial goals, challenges and adjustments to maintain transparency and teamwork.

Sample Bank Account Statement

Commerce Bank Member FDIC

1000 Walnut
Kansas City MO 64106-3686

Jane Customer
1234 Anywhere Dr.
Small Town, MO 12345-6789

	Primary Account Number:	000009752

Bank Statement

If you have any questions about your statement,	Statement Date:	June 5, 2003
please call us at 816-234-2265	Page Number:	1

CONNECTIONS CHECKING Account # 000009752

Account Summary Account # 000009752

Beginning Balance on May 3, 2003	$7,126.11
Deposits & Other Credits	-3,615.08
ATM Withdrawals & Debits	-20.00
VISA Check Card Purchases & Debits	-0.00
Withdrawals & Other Debits	-0.00
Checks Paid	-200.00
Ending Balance on June 5, 2003	**$10,521.19**

Deposits & Other Credits Account # 000009752

Description		Date Credited	Amount
Deposit	Ref Nbr: 130012345	05-15	$3,615.08
Total Deposits & Other Credits			**$3,615.08**

ATM Withdrawals & Debits Account # 000009752

Description	Tran Date	Date Paid	Amount
ATM Withdrawal 1000 Walnut St M119 Kansas City MO 00005678	05-18	05-19	$20.00
Total ATM Withdrawals & Debits			**$20.00**

Checks Paid Account # 000009752

Date Paid	Check Number	Amount	Reference Number
05-12	1001	75.00	00012576589
05-18	1002	30.00	00036547854
05-24	1003	200.00	00094613547
Total Checks Paid			**$305.00**

50/30/20 Budget Planner

Date: _____

Income	Budget	Actual

NEEDS (50% of Income)	Budget	Actual
TOTAL		

WANTS (30% of Income)	Budget	Actual
TOTAL		

SVGS/DEBT (20% of Income)	Budget	Actual
TOTAL		

Notes: _____

_____

_____

_____

Debt Tracker

Date: _____   Starting Balance: _____

Creditor: _____   Monthly Payment: _____

	J	F	M	A	M	J
Paid						
Balance						
	J	A	S	O	N	D
Paid						
Balance						

Date: _____   Starting Balance: _____

Creditor: _____   Monthly Payment: _____

	J	F	M	A	M	J
Paid						
Balance						
	J	A	S	O	N	D
Paid						
Balance						

Date: _____ Starting Balance: _____

Creditor: _____ Monthly Payment: _____

	J	F	M	A	M	J
Paid						
Balance						
	J	A	S	O	N	D
Paid						
Balance						

Using Microsoft Excel

In the realm of finance, various mathematical tools can be employed to calculate monthly payments for loans and credit cards. These calculations are pivotal for both borrowers and lenders to understand the financial implications of borrowing or lending money. A key financial function often used in Excel and other financial software is the PMT (Payment) function.

PMT Function

- The PMT function helps determine the fixed monthly payment required to repay a loan or debt over a specified period at a given interest rate. Its syntax is as follows:

PMT(rate, nper, pv, [fv], [type])

- **rate**: The monthly interest rate (expressed as a decimal). If the annual interest rate is known, divide it by 12.

- **nper:** The total number of payment periods (months) over which the loan will be repaid.

- **pv:** The present value or principal amount of the loan.

- **fv:** (Optional) The future value or final balance. Typically set to 0 for loans.

- **type:** (Optional) Indicates whether payments are due at the beginning (type = 1) or end (type = 0) of each period.

Example 1: Calculating Monthly Loan Payment using PMT Function

Let's say you're taking out a $10,000 loan with an annual interest rate of 6%, to be repaid over 3 years (36 months). The interest is compounded monthly. You can use the PMT function to calculate the monthly payment:

=PMT(0.005, 36, -10000)

The negative sign in front of the result simply means that the payment is an outgoing payment, since you are making a payment on the loan each month.

This calculation gives us a monthly payment of approximately $299.71.

Example 2: Calculating Monthly Credit Card Payment using PMT Function

Credit card balance: $5,000

Annual interest rate: 18% Repayment period: 1 year (12 months)

Convert the annual interest rate to a monthly rate: 18%/12 = 1.5% per month (0.015 as a decimal).

Use the PMT function to calculate the monthly credit card payment:

=PMT(0.015, 12, -5000)

This calculation yields a monthly payment of around $448.77.

Please note that these calculations are based on simplified assumptions and do not consider factors such as compounding frequency or potential additional fees.

For Excel financial functions, go to: https://support.microsoft.com/en-gb/office/financial-functions-reference-5658d81e-6035-4f24-89c1-fbf124c2b1d8

*A special thanks to my grandfather,
Sherif Fawaz Sharaf El-Hashemite, whose love and support,
gives me the courage and confidence to continuously
challenge myself. Your legacy of guidance and
love will forever be woven into these pages.*

Made in the USA
Monee, IL
11 February 2024

53331666R00154